Holy Days

and

Gospel Reflections

Heather King

MAGNIFICAT.

Printed in Canada by Marquis.

Edition number: MGN 20022.

ISBN: 978-1-936260-71-3

Publisher: **Pierre-Marie Dumont**
Editor-in-Chief: **Peter John Cameron, O.P.**
Senior Editor: **Romanus Cessario, O.P.**
Managing Editor: **Catherine Kolpak**
Assistant to the Editor: **Claire Gilligan**
Administrative Assistant: **Nora Macagnone**
Senior Managing Editor: **Frédérique Chatain**
Iconography: **Isabelle Mascaras**
Cover: **Solange Bosdevesy**
Editorial Coordinator and Layout: **Julia Schmidt-Pateu**
Permissions: **Diaga Seck-Rauch**
Translator: **Janet Chevrier**

Preface

To write for MAGNIFICAT *is an assignment I didn't expect and an honor I couldn't have imagined.*

Re-reading these three years' worth of reflections was an interesting exercise. Often the writing seemed entirely new, as if written by another. Often, though I remembered the passage well, I choked up at my own words—not because the writing was so wonderful, but because in their rough way, the words reflected Christ.

I saw where I could have done better, where the writing and thought were clumsy. Afterwards, I sat at my desk and wept. I thought, They are like a lumpy, misshapen cake made by a child!

That's not why I wept, though. I wept because they are still a cake. They are a cake, and they are a cake that perhaps no-one else could have made. They are the fruit of having lost twenty years of my life to alcoholism, of having come to and finding myself with a law degree, of working as an attorney in Beverly Hills, of realizing I was not born for this. In spite of all my wrong turns, I had not lost my child-like heart. That is the surest sign of the Resurrection I know, and when I met the Christ of the Gospels and quit my job to begin writing, I staked my life to it.

MAGNIFICAT *took a chance on me and I am profoundly, for ever, grateful. "But who am I, that the mother of my Lord should come to me?" Elizabeth asked Mary, and that is very much how I feel: about Christ, about Mary, about the Church that has embraced me. Who am I that you should allow me to appear in your pages? Who am I that I should be given this incredible opportunity to spread the Gospels to the end of the earth?*

I have known for twenty-six years that my sobriety is an astonishing, miraculous gift. After seventeen years in the Church, it is just now beginning to dawn on me that everything *is that miraculous, that astonishing, that unmerited. Everything—air, light, life—is that much of a gift.*

Heather King

Los Angeles, August 2013

Table of Contents

O Holy Night:

Advent

First Tuesday of Advent

You Have Hidden These Things from the Wise and the Learned

There was no room at the inn for Mary. Just as would happen today, the innkeeper didn't announce, "Folks, we have a woman among us who is about to have a child, let's a couple of families combine rooms so she can have a bed! Let us keep vigil! Let us fast, then feast!" Just as would happen today, the other guests didn't rise up and say, "O blessed night, O holy night that God has sent this woman among us." They gave her a cursory glance, saw she was poor, said, "Oh—too bad," and sent her to the barn. Just as today, the clerk at the chain motel would say, "Sorry, fifty-nine dollars plus tax," and the rest of us would likely watch Mary trail back to her broken-down van as we go on snacking, texting, and scrolling through our Dish listings.

And yet in our better moments, we carry our little prayer around with us as Mary carried Christ. Like Mary, we're in solidarity with all the poor, all those in exile, all who are powerless, frightened, weak. Like Jesus in today's Gospel, we rejoice that the kingdom is revealed to the childlike.

And just as back then, that prayer moves the world. Just as back then, that prayer is seen by the stars.

Reflection based on Luke 10:21-24

Heavenly Father, help us to remember the miracle that your Son took on human flesh and came into the world as a baby. Help us to be willing, as children are, to live in wonder.

First Wednesday of Advent

The Miracle of the Loaves and Fishes

I don't know about you, but if I'd been healing huge crowds for three days, and it occurred to me they might be hungry, I'd assume they could go to McDonald's and fend for themselves.

Not Christ. In spite of what must have been his own hunger and fatigue, his heart was "moved with pity." Perhaps it was that pity, that heart, that transformed the seven loaves and a few fish into enough food to serve a multitude.

Note that Christ doesn't make the food materialize out of thin air: as always, he invites our contribution, however tiny it might be. Note that he orders the crowd to sit down: things with Christ were never a free-for-all. Note that he first gives thanks: Christ does nothing without the Father. Note that he breaks the loaves: just as his body would be broken on the cross. Note that instead of playing the showman, he lets the disciples distribute the food and garner the accolades: "Wow, thanks, we were starving!" Note that there were leftovers. Note in particular that the miracle of the loaves and fishes follows on three days of healing, and a crowd that has "glorified the God of Israel."

The inevitable manifestation of true healing and true thanks, in other words, is abundance: "good measure, packed together, shaken down, and overflowing" (Lk 6:38).

Reflection based on Matthew 15:29-37

Heavenly Father, when there's enough for me,
help me to remember that there's not enough for someone else.
Open my heart. Help me to share.

Second Monday of Advent

The Paralytic and His Friends

The forgiveness of sins, the parable of the paralytic at Capernaum tells us, is deeply connected to physical healing. What most needs healing, the parable tells us, is the sense of guilt that drives our actions, choices, and relationships. But maybe what the parable really tells us is how to be a friend.

Christ always seems especially partial to those who are willing to risk ridicule in a crowd. Here, the inventive friends are so intent on the healing of their paralytic pal that they clamber up to the roof, perhaps against his protestations—"Come on, fellas, people are gonna think we're *crazy!*"—and lower him down. It's thus the *friends*, with their bold, confident trust in Christ, who are the real stars of the story. It's the friends to whom Christ says, "As for you, your sins are forgiven." He goes on to heal the paralytic physically, but the deeper miracle has already occurred.

How often we assure a troubled friend, "I'll pray for you," then go about our business. How often we are stopped from true prayer by the "derisive crowd" in our own mind. To love one another as Christ loved us is to grab hold of our friend's stretcher, climb on the roof, and say, "Jesus, here, over here! My friend has been stuck in pain for so long! *Please* help."

Reflection based on Luke 5:17-26

Blessed Father, keep me from being discouraged by the lingering paralyses of my friends. Let me come to you for help, so that I may take up my stretcher and go home, too.

Third Sunday of Advent, Year A

Rejoice—and Take No Offense

I once did a forty-day silent retreat. The first time I met with my spiritual director, he asked almost the same question Christ asked his disciples here: "What did you come out to the desert to see?" Did you come to wallow in your weaknesses: a reed swaying in the wind? Did you come to console yourself with your riches: someone "dressed in fine clothing"? Did you come to groom yourself for greatness because you secretly consider yourself a prophet?

In a way, we are all called to be prophets. Like John, we are called to prepare the way for Christ. Like John, in one way we are great and in another way we are the least. And like John, we can look for misunderstanding, persecution, and a deeply unspectacular martyrdom. "Blessed is the one who takes no offense at me."

Sometimes we can't help asking: Why does Christ have to help the blind, the lame, the leprous, the deaf, the dead, the poor? Why doesn't he help *us*—in the way we want to be helped? Why doesn't he make us wealthier, better-looking, more successful?

Because the human heart doesn't rejoice at feeling superior. The human heart rejoices at serving. The human heart rejoices at the truth—which is that we are all leprous, all poor, all dead.

The human heart rejoices at love.

Reflection based on Matthew 11:2-11

Blessed Father, help me to rejoice not as the world rejoices,
but as the kingdom of heaven rejoices.
Help me to take no offense at your Son.

Third Sunday of Advent, Year B

The Voice of One Crying Out in the Desert

Like John in today's Gospel, we don't know who we are. Like John, we walk among people who do not recognize Christ. Like John, we're called to be "out-of-step" with the rest of the world: to be not the light but to testify to the light.

When John was beheaded, Christ must have known something of what was in store for him. People kill you when you point out that their way isn't working. People kill you when you challenge them to examine their purity of heart. Casually, on a whim, they bid some other misguided soul to bring your head on a plate. The magnitude of the crucifixion lies not so much in the hideous violence, but in who and what they were trying to kill. They—and by "they" I mean we—were really trying to kill the Voice: the inner voice that rises again and again, because that is our humanity, and we were made that way by God, and it is the one part of us we can't kill, no matter how hard we try.

In a way, our whole religion consists in acknowledging the voice that cries in the wilderness of our hearts. That voice that wrenches us away from all that is familiar; all that is safe; all that lulls—as the dance of Salomé lulled; all that lies.

Reflection based on John 1:6-8, 19-28

Merciful Father, give us the courage to listen to your voice, no matter where it might lead us. Give us the humility to refrain from wanting to destroy those who challenge us with that which we would rather not hear.

Down in Adoration Falling:

Lent

Ash Wednesday

Praying in Secret

I n today's Gospel, Jesus says, pray in secret. When you fast, don't look gloomy: wash your face, comb your hair, put on a clean shirt. Don't worry about getting praised by the world. God sees your little sacrifices, and "your Father who sees what is hidden will repay you."

Jesus knew human nature well. He knew our tendency toward the wrong kind of martyrdom. He knew our craving to be recognized for our good deeds. He knew how much energy we devote to reacting to the other person, analyzing the other person, and thinking that if only the other person would change, *we'd be all right.* He knew how hard it is, when we are suffering, to refrain from showing that we are suffering.

Al-Anon Family Groups puts out a bookmark called "Just For Today." One paragraph reads, "Just for today I will be agreeable. I will look as well as I can, dress becomingly, keep my voice low, be courteous, criticize not one bit. I won't find fault with anything, nor try to improve or regulate anyone but myself." Al-Anon was founded by and for people who love an alcoholic. That is a kind of perpetual, 24/7 fast. That paragraph in "Just For Today" is exactly what Jesus meant in saying, when you fast, don't look gloomy.

Reflection based on Matthew 6:1-6, 16-18

Most merciful Father, help me to endure my daily slights, distractions, and setbacks without complaining. Help me to refrain from blowing my trumpet of good deeds before me.

First Sunday of Lent, Year A

Led by the Spirit

One reason we need the Church is that, by its nature, Christianity is solitary. I sometimes lament my "exile" as a convert in hipster Los Angeles. But I've traveled to Catholic enclaves, and the people there say they have their own set of challenges. The minute we feel safety in numbers, we tend to start judging. *They only have two kids to our six: are they contracepting?* We don't like to share the limelight. We like to think our security lies in something besides God. God will be our pinch hitter, but for matters of real import, *we'll* be in charge. *We'll* build ourselves up with our reputation as "holy." Depending on our temperament, station in life, and political leanings, *we'll* convert the most people. *We'll* publicly pray the most novenas. *We'll* speak the most "truth to power."

That kind of behavior never authentically converts anyone. What converts, Christ learned in the desert, is a heart that has been purified by inner silence, solitude, and a long, slow crucifixion. As the writer Madeleine L'Engle observes: "We do not draw people to Christ by loudly discrediting what they believe, by telling them how wrong they are and how right we are, but by showing them a light that is so lovely that they want with all their hearts to know the source of it."

Reflection based on Matthew 4:1-11

Heavenly Father, help us to worship God alone.
When we are tempted, send the angels to minister to us.

Thursday of the First Week of Lent

Seek and You Will Find

For a long time I lived in a world where my unspoken thought was, "You go first." You be kind to me and then I'll be kind to you. You be generous with me and then I'll be generous with you. You apologize to me and then I'll apologize to you. Meanwhile I went around thinking, *All I want to do is love! Where is the love! Where is the person I can love?* But really I was thinking, You love me first and then I'll love you. This is the fundamental order that Christ subverts. He makes extraordinary, unconditional promises in today's Gospel: Ask and it *shall* be given. Seek and you *will* find. Knock and the door *shall* be opened.

The way it will be given, found, opened, Christ tells us, is by doing to others whatever we would have them do to us. We let the other guy off the hook and apologize for our own part in a conflict. We try the great experiment and give, not knowing whether the giving will be returned. *We go first.* Knowing the outcome of our actions in advance is fine, but that's a plan. Not knowing and doing unto others because that is good in and of itself—is faith.

Reflection based on Matthew 7:7-12

Almighty Father, give me the strength to continue asking, seeking, and knocking. Help me to persevere, even though the answers seem not to come.

Friday of the First Week of Lent

Paying to the Last Penny

As a lawyer, I often had the opportunity to reflect on Christ's admonition to settle with your opponent on the way to court; otherwise, you will pay to the last penny.

I'll never forget one client, Mrs. Prietto, a widow whose husband had died during surgery, and who'd brought a medical malpractice action against all seven of the doctors involved. Mrs. Prietto was a devout Catholic. Her husband had been choir director at their parish. She attended daily Mass. At her deposition, the opposing lawyer interrupted to sneer, "Have you had any physical complaints since your husband died?" "Physical complaints?" Mrs. Prietto replied, bewildered. "No, it is the little things I miss. Raking leaves together, painting the house…" "I'm asking about *physical* complaints," the attorney snarled. "Insomnia, backaches? Have you been taking prescription medicines since your husband died?" "I don't think you understand," Mrs. Prietto said. "When my husband died it was like I'd been sitting in a brightly lit room and someone, without any warning, snapped the lights off. And they were *never going to come on again.*"

For a second, the room went still. Quiet, soft-spoken Mrs. Prietto had rendered nine attorneys, finally, mute. That was when I saw we were the ones paying to the last penny. Mrs. Prietto didn't need an attorney. In some strange, reverse way, she had already won.

Reflection based on Matthew 5:20-26

Merciful Father, help us to learn to reconcile with our brothers and sisters before we offer our gifts. Help us to settle with our opponents without doing violence to ourselves.

Third Sunday of Lent, Year A

Leaving Our Water Jar

"Rabbi, eat," the disciples say, but Christ seems lost in thought. "I have food to eat of which you do not know." My food is to do the will of the one who sent me. My food is to finish his work. Christ must be drained, hungry, thirsty, hot, but he seems unaware of, momentarily beyond, those things. He is in unity with the Father. He is gathering crops for eternal life.

Is any feeling richer, deeper, more nourishing than the feeling of seeing someone else come awake and alive in our presence? Is there any time we are less aware of ourselves and more willing to lay down our lives for another? Is there any time we are more likely to think, "Maybe God really *is* on my side?"

Later in John's Gospel, Christ says, "How can you say, 'Show us the Father'?…. The words that I speak to you I do not speak on my own. The Father who dwells in me is doing his works" (Jn 14:9-10). Have we even begun to grasp that if we have seen Christ, we have seen the Father? Have we even begun to grasp that it is the Father sitting by that well, too?

Reflection based on John 4:5-42

Almighty Father,
help us to remember that you are as close
as our own thirsting hearts.
Lead us to the living water of Christ.

Third Sunday of Lent, Year B

Christ Understood Human Nature Well

"Jesus…did not need anyone to testify about human nature. He himself understood it well." So ends the passage in John where Christ drives the money changers out of the Temple.

Jesus knew our tendency toward self-serving, dishonest schemes. He knew how willing we are to sell our own souls and the souls of those around us for thirty pieces of silver. But most of all he knew that to attach the name of God to our schemes is infinitely more corrupt than the rough honesty that says, *I know I'm doing wrong and I'm willing to pay the consequences.*

Matthew, the tax collector, was willing to extort money from his fellow citizens, but he was also willing to do so out in the open, ruin his reputation, and suffer the vilification of his neighbors. Much less susceptible to conversion is the secretive, shadowed heart that pretends to act from love but serves a different master. Much more reprehensible is the attempt to mask our craving for security, property, and prestige with a "spiritual" motive. Much more dangerous is the love of money so overriding that it reduces our very bodies to a marketplace: for pharmaceutical companies, for scientific "progress," for sex.

Let us instead be like the penitent sinner in Luke's Gospel who kneels at "the temple" of Christ's feet weeping, caressing his feet with her hair.

Reflection based on John 2:13-25

Eternal Father, may we treat our own bodies,
and the bodies of others, as temples of the Holy Spirit.

Fifth Sunday of Lent, Year C

Woman, Where Are They?

Today's Gospel is the story of the adulterous woman, where Christ tells the crowd: Let him who is without sin cast the first stone. Betrayal, the substance of adultery, is universally recognized as a cut to the core of the human heart.

To side with this deeply marginalized figure, against and in front of the Pharisees, must have put Christ in terrible peril. Christ is all invitation, but he never minces words either. When the baby is about to put his finger in the electrical socket, we don't initiate a discussion; we yell, "No!" Thus Christ saves the adulterous woman and he also says, "Go, and from now on do not sin any more." Neither do I condemn you, but cut it out, now. Otherwise, you will never begin to reach the desire of your own heart. Otherwise, we will both be in trouble.

We are all the adulterous woman, and we are all the people who want to stand in a safe, secure circle and throw stones. If we have not literally committed adultery, we have betrayed and we have known we betrayed. If we have not literally picked up a stone, we have publicly condemned another for a wrong we have done many times privately ourselves. Our sins have been forgiven. To sin no more means to go and not to judge anyone else.

Reflection based on John 8:1-11

Eternal Father,
help me to remember the infinite mercy
you continually show me.
Help me to be merciful to everyone else.

Monday of the Fifth Week of Lent

Left Alone with Christ

Nothing could have outraged the Pharisees more than the company Christ kept. Who is he? they asked. Why has he courted censure, persecution for the sake of an adulteress? "Woman, where are they?"

In this moment of deep intimacy, Christ brings the adulterous woman into relationship with himself. A kind of annunciation, bringing new life. "Has no one condemned you?" "No one, sir." How often the condemning voices are the ones in our head. How often we are divided against ourselves: the pleasure-seeking, self-seeking half ready to stone the other half—our holy longing, our deepest desires—to death.

Christ was tender, but he was never a pushover. He never allowed himself to be manipulated, fooled, or cajoled. Make no mistake about it: you're sinning. "Go and sin no more." Did he and the adulterous woman walk off together? The sense is that she left and Christ stayed, perhaps pondering those mysterious words he had scribbled in the dust.

The parable invites us to picture her walking slowly home, the way we walk as we leave the confessional. Heads bowed. Consciences relieved, for now, of the terrible burden of guilt. Praying with the adulterous woman, "Let it be done unto me according to your Word." Longing with our entire being to become worthy of the promises of Christ.

Reflection based on John 8:1-11

Eternal Father, help us to refrain from casting the first stone.
Let us pray for the purification of our own hearts, bodies,
and minds.

Monday of Holy Week

Stealing the Contributions

Christ loved the poor but Christianity has nothing in it of the pinched, the self-depriving, the dreary. Surrendering the Depression-era mentality I inherited from my beloved parents has been one of the biggest challenges of my spiritual life. I never really knew whether I wanted to go to an Ivy League school, whether I wanted children, whether I wanted to own a house: such incipient desires were stopped dead in their tracks by the thought: *There won't be enough money.* And because I believed there would not be enough money, there often has not been enough money. There wouldn't have been enough money no matter how much I had, because I would have been afraid to spend it: lest none came in to take its place; lest "God" think I was greedy.

All my life poverty has been mistakenly connected in my mind with goodness. Good people are poor, decent people are poor, holy people are poor. For those of us with a compulsion to hoard—the worst form of greed—this is a dangerous thought. I professed to want to be in solidarity with the poor, but I was "stealing the contributions." I was stealing from myself.

It's the last thing we want to admit, and the last thing we allow ourselves to see: sometimes the poor is us.

Reflection based on John 12:1-11

*Heavenly Father, help me to refrain from hiding
a bad motive under a purportedly good one.
Help me to believe there will be enough.*

Angels and Saints:

Holy Days

The Epiphany of the Lord

A Religion Born of Dreams

The Magi appear. The star hovers in the east. The star that points both heavenward to God, and earthward to a family. The Holy Family. Mother, father, child. The family, soon to be on the run, hunted by brutal murderers. The family, perpetually under siege. The family, our sanctuary and our exile. The family, fount of all that is good in us, and all that can become so terribly wounded.

Right from the beginning, Christianity is "a religion you could not have guessed," as C. S. Lewis observed. "It has just that queer twist about it that real things have." The Savior of the universe born with a bounty on his head. The Lamb of God, fresh from the womb, already up against Satan's powers and principalities. Christianity is never sentimental, even toward babies. Joseph and Mary already had in their midst the cross. The infant Christ already had in his eyes the reflection of Mount Calvary.

Christianity has at its center joy, but joy is born of brokenness, limitation, tension, paradox. The shepherds, who have never left their pasture; the wise men, who have traveled from afar. A God of drama, of theater, of sensuality, of extremes: light and dark, poverty and wealth, anguish and hope. In the humblest of dwellings, three Magi materialize bearing gifts: gold, and frankincense, and myrrh; the sweet fragrance of incense. What must Mary and Joseph have thought? What could such an event have signified?

A religion born of dreams: the angel Gabriel who appeared to Mary; the dream of the wise men in which they are warned to return home by another route; the dream of Joseph, as soon as the Magi depart. The dream of every human heart: to love and to be loved; not to die alone. "The star was seen by everyone but not everyone understood its meaning," notes Cromatius of Aquileia in his commentary on Matthew's Gospel.

The Epiphany. The star that sheds just enough light so that we can take one more step, and then we must look to the star again. So like our lives which we, too, live in exile and fear, but also in hope. So emblematic of the strangeness of Christianity; its incongruities and contradictions. Never what we think it's going to be, never what we think we want it to be. Always a fresh twist, a new pain, a new joy. Always a God whose ways are not our ways. Always, just when we think we've found a foothold, the order to flee to Egypt.

The star shines in the east. How quiet the night must have been all around them. How deep the dark.

"God is at home," observed thirteenth-century mystic Meister Eckhart. "We are in the far country."

The Conversion of Saint Paul the Apostle
January 25

Radical Transformation

"Saul, Saul, why are you persecuting me?" (Acts 9:4). Authentic conversion always comes from realizing that we have been "persecuting" Christ.

In the fall of 1986, I spent thirty days at an addiction treatment center in rural Minnesota. Hiking trails meandered through the woods. The trees were turning color. One morning I crept out for a walk just past dawn. Not another soul stirred. I came upon a pond and, through the mist, saw a blue heron, standing stock-still, noble head erect. I saw the heron and the heron saw me.

It was a moment from the Song of Songs, a moment of liminal space and time, an instant of such heart-stopping beauty that in my memory it has attained the level of myth. All those years while I'd been in the bars, this heron, or one like him, had been coming to the pond. All those years while I'd been drinking morning Sea Breezes at Boston's Sullivan's Tap, another parallel world had been breathing, suffering, praising God. Many years passed before I discovered Christ, and more years after that before I came into the Church. But in a way I can mark my conversion from that moment. In a way that heron was Christ, saying, "Heather, Heather, why are you persecuting me?"

Saint Paul fell off his horse, but Christ comes in the form of a lamb, a dove, a heron. That's not to say he's always gentle. But he's often gentlest when we've been doing terrible violence to ourselves and others. Christ never cuts us down with a gun or a sword. He looks at us with love. He says, look at these blue-gray feathers. He says, isn't it lovely to be still and listen to the frogs? He looks us in the eye with love and says, "Why are you persecuting me?"

To be forgiven when we know we don't "deserve" to be forgiven is radically transformative in a way that violence can never be. To be forgiven does another kind of violence: to our whole tit-for-tat notion of crime and punishment. To be forgiven makes us realize that, unbelievable as it may seem, God needs us for something. We have a mission.

My experience with the heron wasn't a white-light experience. It was a door opening onto what has proved to be a long and very slow spiritual awakening of, as William James put it, "the educational variety." How often I've forgotten the heron. How often I've been harsh, rageful, importunate, intolerant, unfaithful, unkind, and just plain wrong.

When that happens I'm struck blind for a few hours or days or even months. Often a long time passes before I see that, once again, I've been persecuting Christ.

Our offense doesn't lie in breaking a rule. It lies in offending against love, against truth, against beauty. What's remarkable about Saint Paul isn't that he had a white-light experience. What's remarkable is that he retained his fervor for all the remaining years of his life.

The Presentation of the Lord
February 2

A Dwelling Place of God

"And you yourself a sword will pierce so that the thoughts of many hearts may be revealed," Simeon told Mary. Whatever pierces our heart is a religious experience. Whatever pierces our heart we are invited to offer at the temple.

We bring all our joys and all our trials. We especially bring our contradictions, our compulsions, our wounds.

To present our experiences at the temple is to sacramentalize them. To present our experiences is to recognize that all experience, from the smallest to the largest, has a supernatural dimension. We offer our experiences on the altar of the fact that we are loved just as we are, and that everything that happens to us is an opportunity to draw closer to Christ. We present ourselves at the temple because our lives, our work, our sacrifices are not our own.

Before we present ourselves at the temple, we see ourselves through the eyes of the world. After we present ourselves at the temple, we see ourselves through the eyes of God.

Outside of the temple, for example, I'm an aging spinster, alone and unloved. Inside, I'm a woman rich in insight, wisdom, and friends; I'm reminded that I have a unique and special task. Before we "present" our drug-addicted son at the temple, we are crazy with worry. We feel like failures as parents, that our life's work has gone for naught. After presenting him at the temple, we remember that we have given our very best, that love is never wasted or lost, that our child is in the hands of God. In fact, that is exactly what Mary and Joseph did with Jesus.

We bring our wounds and we also bring our strengths and talents. Otherwise we tend to forget that the purpose of our gifts is to glorify God. We start to think that our gifts make us special, or that we can use them to lord it over the rest.

When we do present ourselves, we find that the temple is not empty. Simeon is there, and the elderly prophetess Anna. People have been praying for us all our lives. We are part of a centuries-old tradition, and we are invited to participate in the ever-unfolding and perpetual resurrection.

We go in peace, knowing that we, too, are servants whose eyes have "seen your salvation." We, too, are granted a share in showing forth the light of revelation.

"So then you are no longer strangers and sojourners… Through [Christ] the whole structure is held together and grows into a temple sacred in the Lord; in him you also are being built together into a dwelling place of God in the Spirit" (Eph 2:19-22).

Our experiences are "young." The wisdom is old.

Ash Wednesday

Our Relationship to Suffering

My friend Tensie runs a free clinic for farm workers on the central coast of California. She once told me of a young Hispanic woman named Claudia who was dying of cancer; whose heart was broken at the thought of leaving her two-year-old daughter; whose patient endurance, love, and lack of self-pity were exceptional.

"In our culture," Tensie observed, "we view suffering as an insult, a humiliation. The people I see at the clinic suffer terribly, but they don't view it as an insult. They see it as inevitable, as natural almost. In a way, to follow Christ is to examine our relationship to suffering."

Ash Wednesday marks the season in which we especially ponder our relationship to suffering. Praying, fasting, and giving alms are not arcane holdovers from a time when people more inured to suffering than we are found such practices easy. Fasting has always been hard. Fasting is a reflection of the fact that the more desperate we are, the more open we are to change. Fasting reminds that the more keenly aware we are of our empty hands and our empty stomach, the more likely we are to realize we need help. Fasting helps us to remember that we are all poor, and how very much we do not want to be poor.

I'll do anything to keep from feeling "poor" myself, and as Lent approached last year, I thought: *Those people who say fasting is just an ego-based endurance test are right. This*

*year, I'm going to fast in a way that effects some real good.
I am going to fast from criticizing people...*

Ash Wednesday dawned, I waited to be transformed, and within an hour I was mentally nitpicking, criticizing, and judging any number of folks. A few days later I badmouthed someone out loud, the day after that I nakedly passed on a bit of juicy gossip, and from there the whole enterprise rapidly went downhill. Nice try, but unh-unh, I realized. Prayer without fasting is a gesture. Mercy without fasting is a gesture. Fasting is not a gesture. Fasting is a consent to be consumed.

To be consumed by the fire of our own sin leaves cold, dead ashes. To be consumed by the fire of Christ's love is to have our delusions about ourselves consumed and to have our true selves left intact, like the burning-bush love that Claudia, who died at twenty-four, left behind for her daughter.

All through Lent a slow, underground fire burns, to burst into flame with the glory of the Resurrection on Easter morning. *Remember you are dust, and to dust you shall return.* And oh, what hangs in the balance during that interval between the day of our births and the day of our deaths, when for a cosmic instant we, too—beggars all—are called to burst into flame.

Saint Joseph, Spouse of the Blessed Virgin Mary
March 19

The Cross of Family

As a child, when my father was worried, I was worried. There were eight of us kids and, like him, I took every family crisis and wasted penny personally.

One night at supper, as happened often, we ran out of milk. "I'll get some more," little Ross offered, and made for the kitchen. Right away, Dad started in. "Don't drop the milk." "For Crimey's sake, don't drop the milk." "Watch out, Ross, whatever you do, don't drop the milk."

Almost inevitably, just as Ross was about to reach the table, he dropped the milk. Milk pooled on the floor. Milk runneled into the kitchen. A stricken, defeated look crossed my father's face. And then, trembling, he bent over and silently buried his head in his hands.

Had we made Dad cry? Had we pushed him over the brink at last? Mom *couldn't* leave. But what if Daddy, fount of all fun, all jokes, all food, shelter, clothing, security, order, warmth, bolted?

Finally my father straightened up. His beat-up hands dropped to his knees. He was still trembling. His face was wet with tears. But finally we realized he wasn't crying. He was *laughing*!

Daddy had laughed. For a moment, all was right with the world. But in a way, I am still sitting at that table with my father. Sitting with him on one side and my mother on the other, sensing while being too young to know the tension that resides at the center of even the best of marriages. Sitting with him, knowing that when and if he lifted his head his family, his glory and his cross, was going to be looking back at him: waiting, bereft. Sitting with him as he perhaps contemplated the years stretching ahead: of waking in the dark; of standing in the bitter cold and scorching heat all day laying brick; of constant anxiety, constant frustration, constant fatigue. Sitting with him while, on some terrible battlefield in which our fates hung in the balance, all that was good and kind and decent in him, and all that was fearful and weak and in pain had perhaps met.

That silence is the silence of Saint Joseph who, in the Gospels, never utters a single word. Saint Joseph, the husband of Mary, who chose his family, again and again, over himself. Who chose humor—for what good husband and father doesn't have a sense of humor?—over despair, over death. Who today resists the advances of the attractive young girl at work though sorely tempted, who lets his wife take credit for raising such good kids, who stays instead of bolting, which is hard and has always been hard and always will be hard. We say Mary is humble but perhaps the only person more humble, more burdened, less thanked, was Joseph.

In a way, that is who I write for: Saint Joseph, and all husbands like him. For my father, in that moment before he lifted his head—and stayed.

The Annunciation of the Lord

The Invisible Made Visible

S everal years ago I attended an exhibit at L.A.'s Armand Hammer Museum entitled "The Invisible Made Visible: Angels from the Vatican." There were outsized cherubim and huge seraphim but one small bronze, in a badly-lit corner, captivated me. The sculpture consisted of two spare figures, about three feet high: their slender necks extended toward each other like gazelles, their heads tilted, as if listening to music. They both wore long swirling robes and had something in the back that could have been wings, and one wore a kerchief that streamed out straight, as if the figure were leaning into a stiff wind.

The effect was of interactive movement, as if the two were circling both in wonder and tension. Who was the artist who had managed to convey such lightness through the heavy medium of bronze? What did the figures represent? My eyes moved to the placard on the wall: "Virginio Ciminaghi: *The Annunciation*, 1967."

The Annunciation. Of course! I could feel it then, the silence between them, the way everything hinged on Gabriel's earth-shattering question: whether Mary, a poor, uneducated, virgin, would consent to bear the Son of God. The whole cosmos must have stood still, even the trees and stars holding their breath, waiting for her reply.

And then she had said it. She had said it! "Be it done unto me according to Thy word." Not man's word, but the Word of God. Not a life free of suffering, because no such life exists, but a life in which suffering is freely accepted as part of an ongoing creation we are not given to understand fully. Not subservience, but an act of faith so pure that the very atoms of the universe must have momentarily parted.

Transported, I realized I wasn't entirely sure which figure was which. I began circling the sculpture, examining them from every angle, studying the jut of a chin, the bend of an elbow, round and round until I was dizzy, until I realized that we are all both Gabriel and Mary, that we are all both messengers and carriers of the Holy Spirit, that the three of us were *dancing*. We were outside time and space, we were soaring in an ascending spiral, we were making 360-degree turn after impossible 360-degree turn, with no visible means of support.

In *The New Man*, Thomas Merton wrote: "Everything hinges on the final issue, in the battle of life and death. Nothing is assured beforehand. Nothing is definitely certain. The issue is left to our own choice… Are we strong enough to continue choosing life when to live means to go on and on with this absurd battle of entity and nonentity in our own inmost self?"

By myself, I'm not. But the Annunciation reminds me that with faith, which is to say with love, all things are possible. Because this is the paradox of what happened after Mary said yes: everything turned out wrong—and, then again, everything turned out right.

Easter Sunday of the Resurrection of the Lord

A Retinue Advances

One of the most poignant aspects of the Passion is that, beginning in Gethsemane, Christ was stripped of even his privacy. While before he had gone to a lonely place to pray, he now in his naked need "fell on the ground" and prayed before his disciples. He who had always spoken to God in secret now begged, within their hearing, "My Father, if it is possible, let this cup pass from me; yet, not as I will, but as you will" (Mt 26:39).

He had been given to know that he would have to go up to Jerusalem, and be killed, and that he would rise on the third day. But could knowing he would rise have diminished his agony? We, too, "know" we will rise. But unlike us, he did not have the image of the stone rolled away, the empty tomb, the risen Christ. He had not gone before himself. Unlike us, he had no companion, no forerunner, no heart-wrenching Gospel story (Jn 20:11-18) of Mary Magdalene meeting him in the garden: Mary! Rabbouni.

Noli me tangere. Don't touch me. I haven't yet ascended to the Father, and perhaps he also said, "Don't touch me" because the wounds were still fresh and to put pressure on them would have hurt.

To over-focus on the violence of the crucifixion, however, is to miss its essential point. No violence we could re-enact could come close to the Passion of Christ—not because we can't imagine the violence, but because we can't imagine Christ's heart. Christ doesn't keep score, count the cost, or hold the crucifixion against us. The crucifixion was Christ's labor, and just as no loving mother would show her child a gory video of her labor—"Look what I endured for you!"—the writers of the Gospels sketch in the outline and leave the details to our imagination.

That is neither to diminish nor to fail to take full account of the violence. But we don't honor the crucifixion by feeling guilty that Christ died for our sins. We honor the crucifixion by consenting to be stripped down and to die for love ourselves.

Still, what if we could see that when we are cruel to people, we are pressing against the wounds of Christ? What if we could picture each other as survivors of some botched crucifixion: all of us picking our way among the ruins of Golgotha, foraging for a crust of bread and a drop of wine? What if we could realize that everyone is walking around naked with a battered crutch, a dingy bandage over one eye, an arm in a makeshift sling?

In "You Whose Name," Polish poet Czeslaw Milosz imagines the final defeat of death. "A retinue advances in the sunlight by the lakes./ From white villages Easter bells resound."

Saint Mark, Evangelist
April 25

Running Away Naked

S aint Mark's account of Christ's Passion contains a detail not found in either of the other two synoptic Gospels. A crowd has appeared with swords and clubs. Christ has been led away. The disciples have fled. "Now a young man followed him wearing nothing but a linen cloth about his body. They seized him, but he left the cloth behind and ran off naked" (Mk 14:51-52).

I've always had a soft spot for this anonymous young man: bewildered, frantic. Christ, by contrast, his whole ministry moved through the crowds suavely, smoothly. "All the crowd came to him and he taught them. As he passed by, he saw Levi…sitting at the customs post. He said to him, 'Follow me.' And he got up and followed him" (Mk 2:13-14). A great multitude presses in and, typically resourceful, Christ tells his disciples "to have a boat ready for him…so that they would not crush him" (Mk 3:9). He periodically replenishes himself by going off to a "lonely place" to pray. He is never at a loss for words. He never utters a superfluous word. He comes and goes as he pleases, fully in accord with the Father's will.

The rest of us try to follow, and the world clutches at us. The rest of us lurch and falter and run around in circles, making fools of ourselves. Christ offers himself up to be stripped; the rest of us have our "linen cloth" ripped off: torn between our desire for security, certainty, and approval, and the perilous Way of Christ.

Some biblical scholars hold that the naked young man was Mark himself. Mark would presumably have been present at the Last Supper, which tradition also holds took place in the house of his mother. He certainly accompanied Saint Paul to Antioch; he may or may not have gone on to Asia Minor. He may have become the bishop of Alexandria. What we do know is that he reduced the sermons of Paul to writing and left us one of the four Gospels: the shortest, the pithiest, the one that contains the phrase "and immediately" forty-two times.

While the Gospel of Mark ends canonically at 16:20, many biblical scholars suggest that Mark's writing of the Gospel ends, rather abruptly, at verse 8. Luke's Gospel ends with the disciples back at the Temple in Jerusalem, continually praising God. Matthew's Gospel concludes with Christ saying, "And behold, I am with you always, until the end of the age." John ends with, "I do not think the whole world would contain the books" [that could be written about all that Christ did].

Somehow the way Mark ends corroborates for me that he was indeed the young man who ran away naked, that he was one of us.

Mark ends like this: "Then they went out and fled from the tomb, seized with trembling and bewilderment. They said nothing to anyone, for they were afraid."

Blessed Mary, Ever Virgin

The Greatest Saint

"At the cross her station keeping/ Stood the mournful Mother weeping/ Close to Jesus at the last." Thus runs the thirteenth-century Latin hymn known as the *Stabat Mater*: "The mother was standing."

Still standing. Through giving birth in a stable: still standing. Through a prophecy that her heart would be pierced by a sword: still standing. Through watching from the foot of the cross as her Son was tortured to death: still standing. In the three to fifteen years she purportedly lived after Christ died: still standing, still believing, still finding joy and meaning.

Mary, who probably couldn't read but who took care of the baby and cooked the meals, is our greatest saint. To be a mother is to stretch yourself as far as you can possibly go. It is to say, *There! That is everything I have; that is my blood, my heart, my bone marrow.* And it is then to be called to give in yet a different way, a different direction. Just when the mother wants to rest, she is called to more openness of heart, more self-emptying, more patience, more work, more letting go, more love…

Mary knew better than anyone, next to Christ himself, the suffering of the cross. For a mother to witness the brutal execution of an innocent Son—the fruit of her deepest procreative urge, the object of her most profound self-giving—is perhaps the most excruciating form of suffering a woman can endure. A mother would die for her child; Mary watched her child die for her.

"Mary was the Mother Incarnate and her sacrifice was quite simply the complete acceptance of that which happened to her Son, which meant the death of every shred of possessiveness," writes Dante scholar Helen M. Luke.

The death of possessiveness; the birth of God. "My soul doth magnify the Lord," Mary sang, heavy with child, as she journeyed to visit her cousin Elizabeth in "the hill country." What simplicity. What confidence. What humility. What purity—for in order to magnify God, you have to become transparent yourself.

We are all so afraid of falling through the cracks, of being forgotten, of aging, of dying. But if you don't want to be forgotten, we learn from Mary, value your soul more than success or riches or fame. Serve Christ instead of yourself. Become a model of creative suffering, patient endurance, and the erotic urge channeled, contained, and focused into a white-hot flame.

For purity endures. It is Mary who is venerated throughout the world, from the lowest places to the highest, not Cleopatra. It is Mary to whom we pray the rosary, not Marilyn Monroe. It is Mary to whom we appeal for help, for comfort, for solace, for understanding, not Salome.

Every follower of Christ spends a long "December"—maybe many Decembers—in a stable. But May means to burst, with Mary, ever Virgin, into our fullest, most fecund flower.

The Visitation of the Blessed Virgin Mary
May 31

Broken by Love

S eize the Day, a 1986 film based on the Saul Bellow novel of the same name, put the phrase *carpe diem* into public consciousness. For a while we all heard, *Carpe diem!* Seize the Day! Underlying the Visitation is a different message: Receive the Day...

Mary brought herself over the hill country—body, spirit, and soul—to give, but perhaps more importantly, to receive. The same was true of Elizabeth. Many of us are better at giving than at receiving. Giving allows us to maintain a level of control, but to receive requires a vulnerability that can be terrifying.

Several years ago I underwent a shattering, excruciating, falling-in-love experience. I felt as if I were being brought incandescently, electrically alive and at the same time killed. I was stricken. I wept, thinking, *I've been brought to bring love into the world, like Mary, when the angel Gabriel appeared!* I couldn't contain all I felt. I wanted to flee to the hill country, the way Mary fled to Elizabeth, and tell the whole world.

That my love was not returned made the situation even more absurd and several degrees more agonizing, but what would turn out to be a years-long dark night of the soul also turned out to be a religious experience. I was just sane enough to see the tragicomedy of my plight, but eventually I also realized that I was bearing love into the world in the last way I would have chosen, and that to bear love into the world hurts. To love, even if unrequited, is to receive, and to receive is a labor, in every sense of the word. The more intense our holy longing, the more we are broken open, dislodged from our usual "home," torn asunder in pain and joy.

To see that the most bewildering, searingly painful experience of my life was also the gift of my life took many years. To "receive" the deaths of John the Baptist and Jesus must have taken Elizabeth and Mary many years, too. Mary and Elizabeth are both pregnant with sons who will die brutal, barbaric deaths. Both mothers will expand with joy at birth, and will be broken apart, in the harshest imaginable way, when their sons are murdered. But for now, they visit. For now, they share the language of the heart. We visit, we have our moments of communion, and then we go our separate ways: to continue our journeys, to stand at the foot of the cross.

To receive the day requires the heart of a lover, the nerve of a tightrope walker, and the patient, plodding endurance of a pack animal. That is Mary, her heart on fire, traversing the hill country on her way to Mount Calvary. Or as Saint Bernard of Clairvaux observed: "You cannot come to God except by means of Jesus Christ, nor can you come to Christ except by means of his Mother."

The Most Holy Trinity

Co-Equal and Co-Eternal

The Trinity—Father, Son, and the Holy Spirit. Three Persons in one nature. Distinct and yet inseparable. Co-equal and co-eternal.

The Trinity seems to defeat us. Scholars and theologians throw up their hands. Such is the sublime nature of dogma, however, that both the keenest intellect and the heart of the simplest workman are invited to grapple with its depths.

A fisherman can understand that love is the organizing principle of the universe. A carpenter can grasp the miracle that the Son of God—I AM WHO AM—entered human history at a particular time and place. A mother—especially a mother—can understand that reality is undergirded by relationship, community.

The Trinity is not the same as the Holy Family and yet perhaps the Holy Family is one place to start in trying to visualize the relational aspect of the Trinity.

The Father: silent, steadfast; like Saint Joseph, content to stay in the background. The Son: Christ; us. The Holy Spirit: the manifestation of the fact that in the midst of the relationship between any two people is always a third: an energy, a "womb," a new/old "other" that both co-eternally fosters and is co-eternally created by relationship.

Father, Son, and Holy Spirit. There is no room here for violence, competition, jealousy. The Trinity that protects without hovering, that invites without forcing, that keeps itself and each other company, willing to wait an eternity for us to turn toward the light. The God who, though we can't see him, is not an abstraction. The Son who walks, eats, suffers, prays, lives, and dies with us. The Holy Spirit, who is *on our side*. Mary couldn't have said yes to the angel Gabriel unless she knew he was on her side.

"But Mary said to the angel, 'How can this be, since I have no relations with a man?' And the angel said to her in reply, 'The holy Spirit will come upon you, and the power of the Most High will overshadow you'" (Lk 1:34-35).

The Trinity overshadows us. The Trinity is the light in which we see light itself. The Trinity: as mysterious as the seed that falls to the ground, dies, and is reborn as wheat. The Trinity: both unspeakably holy and shockingly simple. The Trinity, that accompanies. In fact, the word "companion" comes from the Latin *cum pane*: with bread.

The Most Holy Body and Blood of Christ

The Inebriation of Love

S omething in us, both light and dark, wants to "experience" blood, a desire that, among so many others, the ritual of Mass fulfills. Birth means blood, death means blood. Getting sober means blood, at least metaphorically.

Above my desk hangs a copy of the Fra Angelico painting *Saint Dominic with Crucifix*, in which the saint is standing at the base of a pedestal with blood from Christ's feet running down in rivulets. The expression on Dominic's face is of wonder, tenderness, pain, which seemed to me to say something very deep about the mystery of love. We want someone to love us enough to shed blood. We want to love deeply enough to shed blood for someone else.

The Real Body. The Real Blood. That we really do have bodies—bodies that hunger, thirst, lust, know cold and heat, get sick, age, die—is the cross. That as incarnate beings we are constantly vulnerable to pain, accident, attack, and insult is the cross. That we bleed real blood when hurt is the cross. The crux of Christianity is that life is *not* an illusion: life is all too real, all the time. If you accidentally drop a baby, if you skate on thin ice, if a drunk driver crashes into your mother, your child, your spouse...

Blood is red, the color of both danger and love; the signal to stop short, the sign of passion and celebration. The *Anima Christi*, an ancient prayer beloved by Saint Ignatius of Loyola, begins:

Soul of Christ, save me,
Body of Christ, sanctify me,
Blood of Christ, inebriate me…

I once stopped in Akron, Ohio, birthplace of Alcoholics Anonymous. By all accounts, AA has saved millions of lives, and I had long been fascinated by the fact that this humble, unlikely enterprise had succeeded—with even one alcoholic—where so many others had failed. Prominently displayed in the office of the archives is a letter from Carl Jung to Bill Wilson, co-founder (along with Dr. Bob Smith) of AA, dated January 30, 1961:

"You see," Jung wrote, "alcohol in Latin is '*spiritus*,' and you use the same word for the highest religious experience as well as for the most depraving poison. The helpful formula therefore is: *spiritus contra spiritum*."

Whether toward the heights or toward the depths, spirit is wine-dark, blood red, and inexhaustibly self-generative. The vampire, his heart black with hate, craves ever to feed on us; as members of the Church, we feed on the heart of Christ, perpetually bleeding with love.

As an alcoholic, sober many years, I fast from partaking of the Blood of Christ. Instead, I approach the chalice with arms crossed, bow my head, and receive a blessing.

Like Saint Dominic, I gaze up at his feet: in trembling, in adoration. Even to come that close to the Precious Blood is to be inebriated.

The Most Sacred Heart of Jesus

The Pulse of Humanity

Recently I was walking to morning Mass in Los Angeles, with the trees and sky above, and the traffic and noise and violence of rush hour below. I kept looking up: to the birds; to a place where I could imagine it was quiet. If you get very quiet, you hear, at the very center of the universe, a pulse, a beat. You hear the birds and the honking horns, the suffering and the joy. You hear the Sacred Heart of Christ.

So in the middle of a city of millions, I decided to pray the rosary.

And praying the rosary after a couple of minutes what I "heard" was the people who are waiting for biopsy results, for the husband to show up, for the electricity to be turned back on, and I saw that these are the people who are sweating tears of blood with Christ in the Garden at Gethsemane.

I heard the tears of the teenage girl who is cutting herself, the child whose psychotic mother is forcing him to hold his hand over a gas stove, the women who are being raped, and these are the people who are being scourged at the pillar with Christ.

I heard the overworked heart of the CEO who opens his inbox to find two hundred messages, the day laborers wielding eardrum-shattering leafblowers for ten hours at a stretch, the twelve-year-old who must translate for her parents when immigration services come to the door, and these are the people who are staggering under the weight of the cross with Christ.

I heard the wife who has just discovered that her husband is having an affair with the housekeeper, the farmer who is forced to sell the generations-old family farm to a conglomerate, the playwright who has poured out his heart and soul and is panned on opening night by the critics, and these are the people who are being crowned with thorns along with Christ.

All over the world, all day, every day, people are suffering, and here comes Barry, the homeless schizophrenic and hopeless alcoholic who wanders Sunset Boulevard, one grimy hand clutching a plastic bag holding his worldly belongings, the other held out in a perpetual plea for booze money. What to do in the face of such suffering? What to do with your brokenness, your weakness, your own suffering and loneliness and fear?

You give Barry a couple of bucks. You make sure to shake his hand and thank him, because this is Christ, and his heart is your heart.

And you keep walking, to Mass.

Saint Mary Magdalene
July 22

Pure Burning Love

S hortly after I was confirmed in 1996, I often attended Sunday Mass at Dolores Mission. Dolores Mission is one of L.A.'s poorest parishes. Inside, the church is dark and cool, with a glass custard dish of holy water, flickering Jesus candles, and plaster statues of the Virgin. The crowd is casual, with lots of children, babies, and strong-looking women. These women look you right in the eye and smile and say, "*La Paz de Cristo*" with such rooted warmth that their faith flows through you like an electric current.

Connie is one of the quieter ones. Connie has the phlegmy cough and emaciated frame of a diehard smoker, and a smile so open and trusting it is a kind of gift. Her long black hair is parted in the middle, and she wears an oversized T-shirt and a small gold cross around her neck. Sometimes she brings her teenage son with her, a hulking acne-scarred youth to whom she seems touchingly devoted.

One Sunday morning before Mass begins, Juanita, one of the ladies of the church, comes by and asks if we'd like to present the gifts.

We regard each other shyly. "I'd be glad to, but I've never done it before," Connie says. "Me either," I echo.

"It's easy," Juanita waves us off. "Just come on back when the time comes and I'll show you what to do."

After the offering, we walk tentatively to the rear of the church. Juanita positions us side by side, hands the pie plate of hosts to Connie and the cruet to me, and gently shoves us toward the aisle.

"It's an honor, isn't it?" Connie says in an awed whisper. Her nail polish is chipped and her eyes are smudged with mascara. "They asked me to do it once before, but I couldn't that day: I was too filled with sin."

I was too filled with sin. The admission alone is courageous enough, but what really grabs me is that, because of it, she declined the honor of touching the bread and wine. In her place, I would have been afraid of being perceived as a snotty Anglo, of hurting someone's feelings by "rejecting" them, of being judged. That I might not be worthy to present the gifts that would be transformed into Christ's Body and Blood would not even have entered my mind. All of my reasons for saying yes would have had to do with pleasing another person. Connie's reason for saying no had been Christ.

People sometimes ask, "How can you be 'spiritual' and live in L.A.?" I want to say, because I once stood on a patch of holy ground in poverty-stricken Boyle Heights, the sun blazing through a cheap stained-glass window of Jesus. Because I once saw Connie—a love bite throbbing on her neck, her mouth an inferno of fuchsia lipstick—making her way to the altar with a pie plate of hosts, her heart on fire with pure burning love.

Because Mary Magdalene lives here.

The Transfiguration of the Lord
August 6

A Profound Inward Light

C hrist leads Peter, James, and John up a high mountain and is transfigured in light. Elijah appears. The disciples are bewildered, transfixed. At a loss for words, Peter impulsively suggests, "Let's set up a booth."

But the message of Christ is not a message that you set up a booth to promulgate.

Christ is not self-effacing. He takes the full measure of himself. He knows exactly who he is and what he is about. But Christ does not advertise. Shining like the sun, white as light, blindingly radiant, Christ simply is. "This is my beloved Son, with whom I am well pleased; listen to him."

In the passage just before the Transfiguration, all three of the synoptic Gospels have Christ saying (with slight variation), "For whoever would save his life would lose it, and whoever loses his life for my sake will find it." And just after the Transfiguration, in Matthew and Mark, he cautions the disciples to tell no one of the vision until the "Son of man" is raised from the dead.

The recounting of the Transfiguration is sandwiched, in other words, by death; by the revelation that Christ has come to transform death. He leads Peter, James, and John up "a high mountain apart," and that is where he leads us as well: to tell us that to save our life is to lose it, to take up our cross; that he will repay every man for what he has done, but that in the meantime the world will repay us with scorn, derision, and persecution.

No advertiser would attach his product to Christ. Christ is the cross. Christ is God united to us in our suffering. Christ does not have a message to sell; he has himself—to offer up completely to the Father. To try to market Christ would be to try to market the deepest cry of our hearts. To try to market Christ is to try to market what takes place on a marriage bed—or a deathbed.

As always, Christ is both astonishing and everyday; both exactly what we want and exactly what we don't want. He reveals himself in private, knowing that he will die in public. He reveals himself only to highlight that the Way is by its nature hidden, silent, invisible, anonymous.

Christ is transfigured; inwardly on fire, we appear to the folks around us as the same humdrum people we always have been. As Charles Péguy observed, "The Christian, Christianity, Christendom, is not a public operation, a superficial, historical operation: it is not a public event. It is a secret event, a profound inward operation, and often, the more profound it is the less it modifies external aspects and appearances."

The Passion of Saint John the Baptist
August 29

The Scandal of Christianity

"He must increase; I must decrease," observed John the Baptist (Jn 3:30). What does that mean? What does "decreasing" look like in daily life?

To decrease doesn't mean being a doormat, but it does mean that we stop fighting anybody and anything, even evil. "Resist not evil," said Christ: in other words, let's not waste our energy fighting. Let's use our energy to learn how to love. Let's use our energy reflecting on the strangeness, the astonishment, the upending nature of Christ.

The scandal of Christianity—that the antidote to violence is not more violence, but love—is so extreme, so radical, that in two thousand years we have not begun to accept it. Our egos can't bear such meager results, such plodding slowness, such invisibility.

Then, as now, people were butchered for a trifle: an obscene dance; the whim of a call girl. Then, as now, the voice calling us to come awake was demeaned, devalued, snuffed out. "Love your enemies, and pray for those who persecute you," Christ taught (Mt 5:44). The world, then as now, plots to kill Christ.

John, a voice crying in the wilderness, proclaimed: "Repent and believe the Good News." And the Good News, almost unbelievably—the antidote to the mindless brutality that would kill first him, then Christ—is to love one another as Christ loved us. Wishing people well in our hearts, especially people who have hurt us. Letting people off the hook. Saying, "I'm sorry"; when appropriate, saying, "No," saying, "Come higher, friend." Transforming our anger, rather than transmitting it. Praying to be relieved of the desire to be the favorite, to be consulted. Refusing to respond to violence, whether physical, psychological, or spiritual, with more violence. Thérèse of Lisieux, Francis of Assisi, and Maximilian Kolbe understood this Good News well. They died for it. That is why we made them saints.

That the Savior of the world should be proclaimed by a man viewed by the world as a crackpot, who died alone and in ignominy, tells us much about what we can expect for ourselves. The disciples couldn't sit for an hour with Christ in the garden at Gethsemane, but John, in his prison cell, had no one even to ask.

Then, as now, the voice saying, "Look at the violence and dishonesty in your own heart" is the most dangerous voice of all. The most rare. The one we least want to hear. How dare someone tell us we shouldn't sleep with our brother's wife, or cede our sexuality to a pharmaceutical company, or clone a human being.

"The Kingdom of God is at hand." Let us sit for an hour with John. Let us stoop to untie Christ's sandal.

The Exaltation of the Holy Cross
September 14

A Love Affair with Paradox

"My hour is not yet come," Christ said at the wedding feast at Cana, when he performed his first public miracle. That it did come, and that he took the form of a slave, embraced it, and "humbled himself and became obedient unto death, even death on a cross" (Phil 2:8) was the consummation of his life, his love, his work, his obedience, his body, spirit and soul.

As G. K. Chesterton says in *The Everlasting Man*, "We are meant to feel that Death was the Bride of Christ as Poverty was the Bride of Saint Francis of Assisi. We are meant to feel that his life was in that sense a sort of love affair with death, a romance of the pursuit of the ultimate sacrifice."

To lift high the cross is to lift high paradox. The most impenetrable darkness; the most impenetrable light. The grain of wheat that unless it falls to the ground and dies "abideth alone," but if it dies, "it bears much fruit (Jn 12:24). A Savior who said, "Blessed are the peacemakers" and who also said, "I came not to bring peace, but the sword." A call to the hero's journey offered to the small, the broken, the invisible, the cast-aside, the weak. A religion that has spawned untold volumes of theology, ontology, eschatology, and philosophy and that leaves us at the end of time with a single question: "How did you treat the least of these brothers and sisters of mine?"

Only Catholicism could call the day Christ was crucified Good Friday. Only Catholicism says that the highest thing is not health, the highest thing is not even life: the highest thing is love. Only Catholicism could have given us the Repentant Thief—who, hanging on the cross beside him, turned to Christ and said, "Remember me when you come into your kingdom." Only Christ—alone among any God ever conceived, the master who suffers for his servant—could have turned back in his agony, and promised, "This day you will be with me in Paradise."

Not later, when we've become "holy," or "successfully" battled cancer, or become first in someone's heart, but now—in clothing and feeding and visiting each other in prison, in keeping each other company, with all our imperfections and in all our incompleteness, as we suffer, and age, and die. That is how we stand alongside Christ in the cosmic battle between good and evil. That is how we prepare for eternity.

"Thou didst not spurn the Virgin's womb," runs the *Te Deum*. Christ did not spurn the Virgin's womb and he did not spurn to die, before a jeering crowd, with his Mother looking on. It was his hour, and he gave it, to the last drop of blood, to us. Would that when our hour comes, we kneel at his feet and offer every drop of ours back.

Saint Vincent de Paul, Priest
September 27

Embracing the Imperfect

Saint Vincent de Paul (1581-1660) was born into a French peasant family, earned a degree in theology, was captured by Turkish pirates and sold as a slave, escaped with his master, whom he converted, and returned to France. A lesser man might have been embittered or fatally traumatized. Saint Vincent, by contrast, began to work tirelessly for the poor. He had a special charism for galley convicts, who at the time lived in subhuman conditions of pestilence and misery. He opened shelters, soup kitchens, and hospices, first in France, then around the world.

We live in a culture that prizes intelligence. Saint Vincent de Paul was clearly intelligent—to come from a peasant family and earn a college degree is no small feat, in any era—but true intelligence resides in the heart. Intelligence regards the suffering of the rest of the world and realizes, *I'm complicit in it.* Intelligence has a conscience and the hunger to know, *How can I help?* True intelligence embraces and encompasses the imperfect: the blind, the lame, the leper. True intelligence, after years on the rock-strewn spiritual path, comes to the notions of self-renunciation and sacrifice.

That's why, after Christ, the next most intelligent people are the saints. Only the mind of the saint takes in the whole picture. Science—wondrous! Mathematics: sheer beauty, to be studied in depth. Physics! Devote every waking hour to its mysteries if you're so moved—but all to be seen through the lens and put at the disposal of love.

Gregor Mendel, founder of modern genetics, was an Austrian scientist and monk. The Big Bang theory was developed by Georges Lemaître, a Catholic priest. But at the end of the day the question, for each of us, is: *What was my orientation of heart toward the people with whom I came in contact over the last twenty-four hours? How am I treating the people who can do nothing for me? Is my work for my glory or for God's?*

Saint Vincent de Paul saw that one truly intelligent way to follow Christ is to recognize our own spiritual poverty and to serve that poverty in "the least of these." He recognized that one truly intelligent way to practice theology was to tend to galley convicts, untouchables, and incurables.

Three centuries later, the followers of Saint Vincent de Paul still work tirelessly for charity and justice. His name is still synonymous with care for the poor. In twenty-first-century Los Angeles, everyone knows where to send the down-on-their-luck family who needs clothes, pots and pans, or furniture: the football arena-sized Society of Saint Vincent de Paul Thrift Store, over in Lincoln Heights.

When Albert Einstein died, scientists removed, dissected, and meticulously studied his brain. One hundred and seventy years after Saint Vincent de Paul died, the members of the faithful prayed, wept over, kissed, and, with a high Mass, made a relic of his still incorrupt heart.

Saint Thérèse of the Child Jesus,
Virgin and Doctor of the Church
October 1

"I choose all!"

For thirty-seven years, Jeanne McNulty has lived in a holler in Spencer, West Virginia: praying, embracing a simple lifestyle, gardening, gathering firewood, and reaching out to some folks in her rural county by nursing the sick in their homes.

She maintains modest hermitages in the woods there where folks, for a small donation, come to spend time in deep solitude, take long walks, or sit quietly in the straw bale chapel which houses the Blessed Sacrament.

Jeanne is a member of the Order of Consecrated Virgins and she also belongs to the Third Order of Saint Francis.

The first time I visited the hermitage, I immediately knew she was a normal human being with a deep and authentic inner life. First, she came out from her cheery red-painted house to give me a hug. Next, she invited me in, sat me down, and made me a grilled cheese sandwich with home-made pickles. And the minute she found out I was a writer, being a fledgling at the art, she exclaimed, "Really! How do you get an agent?"

At the time I was contemplating writing a book about Saint Thérèse of Lisieux, the virginal French nun who had entered the cloister at the age of fifteen, discovered that "My vocation is love!", and died in agony from TB at the age of twenty-four. Our culture would say of such a life, What a waste! How neurotic! In *The Story of a Soul*, Thérèse's autobiography, I saw something deeper: a freedom, a fierceness. "The Little Flower" was not less passionate than any other beautiful girl her age, but more.

One night Jeanne invited me to dinner. "Have you always wanted to be alone?" I kicked off the conversation. She replied, "I have always felt the call to celibacy and drawn to spend many hours in solitude. Even as a very young girl I sat in the church by the hour, looking and listening, and one day I 'heard'—'I want you.'"

She said, "When I chose a life of solitude in the holler, I didn't feel the prison gates were clanging shut behind me. I felt as if the gates of heaven were opening." The mountains provided the cloistered solitude her heart longed for. She still had her struggles, including occasional loneliness, but hunger for a man wasn't one of them.

"I like men," she continued. "I have many relationships with men, lots of priest friends. It's easy for me to open up to them. But"—a girlish smile spread over her face—"it's him I want. Christ is my all. It sounds strange, I know, especially coming from one such as I. But the fact is that one man wouldn't be enough for me…."

That's a modern-day Thérèse of Lisieux. That's a woman in the fullest flower of self-giving love.

The Holy Guardian Angels
October 2

Bringing Life Out of Death

The assigning of a guardian angel to every person on earth is a cherished notion in Church tradition. Though not rising to the level of doctrine, the concept is in the "mind of the Church" as Saint Jerome put it way back in the fourth century. While originally a local observance, in 1608 the feast was placed by Pope Paul V into the general Church calendar. Today, the Catechism corroborates that "the existence of the spiritual, non-corporeal beings that Sacred Scripture usually calls 'angels' is a truth of faith... 'Beside each believer stands an angel as protector and shepherd leading him to life.' [Saint Basil]" (328, 336).

People felt this way, it turns out, long before Christ.

In Genesis 32, Jacob wrestles with "his" angel. "Angel" means messenger, and this is certainly the way many of us react to a new or strange call.

God tells Moses, "See, I am sending an angel before you, to guard you on the way and bring you to the place I have prepared. Be attentive to him and obey him." (Ex 23:20-21).

My own sense is that invisible hands are constantly saving me from yet another chronic blunder. Steeped in Psalm 91, I was once hiking through the Santa Monica Mountains when I came upon a trail crew, hacking away brush, clearing boulders. "How lovely!" I exclaimed. "Lest I dash my foot against a stone!"

The guardian angels are especially associated with children, and tradition has it that the protectorate begins at birth; before birth, a child is protected by the guardian angel of his or her mother. Such thinking can seem the province of those who also believe in the tooth fairy, but, charming though the notion of a guardian angel may seem, it is entirely in keeping with Christian theology. Like Christ, the guardian angel does not necessarily save from death; but rather helps to bring new life from death. How like our merciful God to see that the soul of the child who is miscarried—even the child who is aborted—continues under the aegis of his or her mother's guardian angel.

The children who died at Auschwitz, the children who are murdered at the hands of a psychotic stranger, the children who suffer all their short lives from a terminal illness remind us that the protection of God is a very different matter than the earthly protection of insurance policies and private schools and armed bodyguards. Before the mother whose child has died or been murdered, we must stand mute. Before the stricken father, and alongside our own guardian angel, we can only plead: "I do believe, help my unbelief!" (Mk 9:24).

How blessed we are, each, to have been assigned one.

Christ alone is guarded by the entire fleet. In the desert with Satan, "he was among wild beasts"—he is still—"and the angels ministered to him" (Mk 1:13).

All Saints
November 1

An Acute Fever

When I told a lapsed friend I'd published a book about Saint Thérèse of Lisieux, she rather pointedly inquired: "But you don't have to be *inside* the Church to be a saint, do you?" I understood her concern; one of my abiding obsessions is the "unsung saint": the person who is never noticed.

But here's why saints are compelling: Saints are exceptional. Saints are *extreme*. As William James observed in *The Varieties of Religious Experience*: "There can be no doubt that as a matter of fact a religious life, exclusively pursued, does tend to make the person exceptional and eccentric... It would profit us little to study this second-hand [i.e., conventional, ordinary] religious life. We must make search rather for... individuals for whom religion exists not as a dull habit, but as an acute fever rather."

So though in the general sense "saints" can be found everywhere, those who love Christ tend to be the most extreme people of all. Thus we have an eleven-year-old who preferred to be stabbed to death rather than yield her virginity (Saint Maria Goretti). We have a nun who drank the pus from the cancerous breast of her mother superior (Saint Catherine of Siena). We have a medieval scholar, regarded as one of the most magnificent philosophers the world has known, who at the end of his life regarded his *œuvre* and remarked, "All straw!" (Saint Thomas Aquinas).

I have my own personal pantheon: Saint Dymphna, patron saint of the mentally ill. Saint André Bessette, who achieved sainthood by humbly tending the door of a Montreal church for forty years. A new favorite is Saint Mark Ji Tianxiang, a Chinese layman and opium addict who was prohibited from receiving the sacraments for the last thirty years of his life because of this "grave sin." During the Boxer Rebellion, in which Christians were brutally persecuted, he was sentenced with many others to die and is reputed to have gone to his execution singing the Litany of the Blessed Virgin Mary.

How capacious a Church that holds to her bosom female saints and male saints; saints of every race, age, demographic, IQ, livelihood, and walk of life! How welcoming the arms of a Church that embraces as some of her most precious children the broken, the fragile, the weak, the still sinning, the still in bondage, the still stuck. How emblematic of a Church of mercy and humor to take us as we are. How wise the Church is to understand that perfection consists not in ridding ourselves of every fault but in our capacity to give and to receive love.

In its original form, "saint" simply meant "friend of Jesus" (Col 1:2). That's what saint still means. Glory be to God that the invitation is extended to all.

The Commemoration of All the Faithful Departed
(All Souls)

November 2

The Freedom of Heaven

A year before my mother died, I went to visit her at the nursing home in Dover, New Hampshire, where she lived.

She was sitting quietly in a chair looking out the window at the sunset. Mom had Alzheimer's, and her responses had become rather broad. "What did you have for lunch, Mom?" "Food." "Who's picking you up for Thanksgiving dinner, Mom?" "Uh...yeah."

"Mom," I said, "it's me! It's Heather. Your oldest child!" Pause. "Oh?"

All my life, I'd worn my emotions on my sleeve; Mom kept hers under wraps. I was always bursting into tears; Mom was always dry-eyed. Before it was too late, I yearned to have the conversation I'd yearned to have all my life. The one where we *bonded*. The one where she said, *How beautiful is your passionate heart!* The one where she said, *You're the daughter I always wanted.*

We talked about my flight from L.A., the weather, our plans the next day for lunch. And then I asked the only question that truly interested me.

"What do you *think* about, Mom?" I asked eagerly. "What goes through your head when you look out the window?"

"I don't know," she replied modestly. "I suppose they keep us so busy I don't have much time to think."

Tremulously: "Do you think about *Daddy*?"

"Oh yes, from time to time. You never forget."

Again, I was overcome by my lifelong desire to "know" my mother; to have her know, see, understand me.

"Mom," I blurted, "do you think after we die that we're *reunited with the people we love*? Do you think afterward *we're all together*?"

"No," she replied shortly. "I think when you go you just go. I just try to enjoy each day as it comes."

My mind raced. Mom, a lifelong Protestant, believed in God: what about the Resurrection? What about the seed falling to the ground and dying and bearing much fruit? What about Jesus appearing to the disciples after the third day?

"Really?" I said. "You don't think there's anything afterward at all?"

"You don't have to worry about that," she waved me off. "That will take care of itself. Let someone else worry for a change."

I looked over at that dear, common-sense face, and I suddenly saw that I must have driven her crazy with my incessant desire to over-bond, over-emote, over-worry. I saw my whole life I'd waited for a conversation that in this world didn't, couldn't, exist. *Enjoy each day as it comes. Let someone else worry for a change.* Everything was all right. Everything had always been all right.

Maybe the greatest gift we can give the people we love, alive or dead, is to free them from our expectations. I will pray for her, and all those I have loved, on All Souls' Day.

But no one, not even Mom, can convince me that we're not going to all be together after we die.

Our Lady of Guadalupe
December 12

A Shower of Out-of-Season Roses

Years ago, I attended a retreat for sober alcoholics led by a priest named Father Bill.

Father Bill combined high intelligence, a black sense of humor, and a tender heart. He'd been educated, among other places, in Rome. He'd studied with the pope. He told of coming back to Southern California and landing at a parish where he'd thought to impart some of his deep theological insights. Instead, the people kept stringing up tinsel, lights, tissue paper cut-outs. Every time he turned around they were loading up the sanctuary with Sacred Heart prayer cards and plastic statues of Mary.

One day at the beach, pondering his dilemma, he set up his chair near a young father and his little girl. The father was trying to nap and the little girl would bring her pail down to the water, fill it with shells, and staggering under its weight, lug the pail back. "Daddy, Daddy! Look!" The father would open one eye, say, "That's nice, honey," and roll over on his other side. The little girl would totter back to the shoreline, fill her empty pail with shells, and drag it back: "Daddy! Daddy!"

Suddenly Father Bill realized this little girl was like the Hispanics at his church. They wanted to throw a party for the Father they loved! They wanted to shower him with trinkets and gifts!

He heard a "voice" saying, "If I want to change the Church, Bill, *I'll* do it."

To be a Catholic in L.A. is to live in the midst of such exuberance: a very real reason why I converted here. To be among people who know how to spend their last pennies on a bunch of paper flowers; who consider it an unthinkable deficit for a woman to be childless (I am childless myself); who think to mark the place on the desert highway where someone has died with a wooden cross has been a great and ongoing gift.

In 1531, the story goes, the Mother of Christ appeared to an Indian convert named Juan Diego, leaving her portrait on Juan Diego's mantle (*tilma*, in Spanish). The *tilma*, now a treasured relic, is housed at the Basilica of Our Lady of Guadalupe in Mexico City, the most visited shrine in the world.

How beautiful that Mary, ever humble, appeared to an unknown farmer. How beautiful that she filled Juan Diego's coarse-fibered *tilma* with an armful of out-of-season roses: a sign of Christ's love, showered back to a people who have so profligately showered theirs upon him.

All around Los Angeles on December 12 will be pageants; Masses; statues of the Virgin, in her blue, star-studded mantle, held aloft. All around, the ground littered with tinsel, voices will be raised in song to *La Guadalupana, La Paloma Blanca,* and *La Magnifica.*

May the strains waft up, God rest his soul, to Father Bill.

The Nativity of the Lord
(Christmas)
December 25

True North

How beautiful Los Angeles is for Christmas! Toyon berries, bright red against dark green glossy leaves. The sharp smells of sage and rosemary. Incandescent sunsets. At dusk, I like to set out for a walk around my Silver Lake neighborhood, which is all hills and secret staircases and blind alleys and dead ends and surprise views. One of my favorite routes is up Marathon Street, down Micheltorena, south across Sunset Boulevard, and then continuing north up all the way to the crest of the hill that is so steep I'm pretty sure it goes through at least one climate change and possibly a time zone. At the very top is a house with an outdoor drop display of tiny Madonna-blue lights, very thrilling after the long climb and showcased against the inky night.

A tiny silver crescent moon. Dead quiet. I think of all the places I've walked in my life—Boston, Paris, New York, Florence, Oaxaca, Fez, Amsterdam, Athens, London, San Antonio, Tucson. Ozona, Texas, Taos, New Mexico. That's not even counting the back roads, the mountains, the deserts, the towns I never knew the names of, because I have a pilgrim heart and so walk wherever I go.

Peering through the occasional lighted window, I think about how I found the pearl of great price—my writing, my life—and sold everything I had and bought it. A life ever so slightly poor in money but rich in silence and solitude; a life with a minimum of noise, distractions, busyness, possessions, and a maximum of time to ponder. A life that has given me legs that walk, eyes that see, the Gospels. A life in which, if I get really quiet, I sometimes seem to feel, just for a moment, the pulse of the whole world.

I've never had a child but looking at the lights of the city spread out below, I'm thinking this is maybe how a mother feels as the time to give birth draws near: a fullness, an expectancy, a sense of not being able to contain all that you feel, all that you know; all that you've been given; all that you want to give in return.

Later I'll drive across the L.A. River to Atwater Village, the evergreens along the median strung with lights, and onto a dark side street to Holy Trinity for 7 PM Mass. As always when I try to make Mass every day, things right themselves. One more time, I find true north, or true north finds me.

Part of me thinks, *I should cook this year. I should make home-made gifts. I should….* But this year, while our mother Mary waits to give birth, I am sitting with another Mary, the sister of Martha, at the knee of Christ (Lk 10:38-42).

This Advent, I have chosen "the good part," and it shall not be taken from me.

My Soul Doth Magnify

the Lord:

Reflections on Luke

Spreading the Message of Love

When the days for his being taken up were fulfilled, [Jesus] resolutely determined to journey to Jerusalem, and he sent messengers ahead of him. On the way they entered a Samaritan village to prepare for his reception there, but they would not welcome him because the destination of his journey was Jerusalem. When the disciples James and John saw this they asked, "Lord, do you want us to call down fire from heaven to consume them?" Jesus turned and rebuked them, and they journeyed to another village. (Lk 9:51-56)

Thus Christ begins his journey to Jerusalem where, nailed to the cross, he will subvert the age-old cycle of eye-for-an-eye, tooth-for-a-tooth, retributory violence. The Jews and Samaritans have been at odds for centuries, just as, our whole lives, we have been at odds with our neighbors, God, ourselves.

Like the disciples, our solution is often to call down fire on our "enemies." Our impulse is to annihilate all who stand in our way. The way of Christ is infinitely gentler and infinitely more difficult. Christ calls us to overlook mercifully the faults of others and to examine fiercely our own. Christ calls us to discover the power of humble charity. Christ calls us to look at the violence within ourselves.

In 1953, a woman named Mildred Lisette Norman gave up all her worldly belongings, took on the name "Peace Pilgrim," and, starting in Pasadena, California, walked for the next twenty-eight years. She walked thousands of miles, crisscrossing the United States: fasting until she was given food, walking until she was given shelter, speaking to all who would listen about peace. "This has been our trouble down through the ages—we have given only lip service to Christian values, and lived by the jungle law of tooth and claw," she observed. "We have quoted '*Be not overcome of evil, overcome evil with good*' and then attempted to overcome evil with more evil, thereby multiplying the evil."

Christ knows that we are never converted by violence. We are converted by being accepted: all the good and all the bad. We are converted by being welcomed, by being invited to contribute our gifts, by being willing to be called to our highest selves. We don't convert others by telling them they are wrong; we convert others by showing them Christ.

"Who are you?" his disciples ask him (Jn 8:25). And in reply, Christ asks, over and over again: Who are *you*?

Heavenly Father, help me to refrain from calling down fire on my enemies. Teach me to turn to you for help with the many things that I can't do by myself.

Nowhere to Lay Our Heads

As [Jesus and his disciples] were proceeding on their journey some-
one said to him, "I will follow you wherever you go." Jesus answered
him, "Foxes have dens and birds of the sky have nests, but the Son of
Man has nowhere to rest his head." And to another he said, "Follow
me." But he replied, "[Lord,] let me go first and bury my father." But
he answered him, "Let the dead bury their dead. But you, go and
proclaim the kingdom of God." (Lk 9:57-60)

One of the great temptations for a follower of Christ is to come up with a formula. Publishers like authors to have a "platform." We want a foothold from which to dispense spiritual wisdom. We strive for bullet points and a brand.

I once watched a documentary on Dietrich Bonhoeffer, the Lutheran minister and prisoner of conscience during the Nazi regime. One scene was a clip of Hitler before a maniacally enthusiastic crowd, shaking his fist at God and saying, "We're ready! We're in control! We have a plan! *Now bless it!*" Later the camera panned to a photo of Bonhoeffer, taken at a family gathering during the time when he and several of his male relatives were plotting to assassinate Hitler. The contrast was striking. While Hitler's face bore the bloodless, single-minded stare of the fanatic, Bonhoeffer's was marked by uncertainty and conflict. That's just it: as followers of Christ, we don't get to have a foothold. Like him, we have nowhere to lay our heads.

To be a follower of Christ means being certain that we are to love each other as he loved us, and being very uncertain what that means in any given situation. It means being certain that the light will prevail, and then consenting to walk in almost complete darkness. It means being certain about Christ, and very, very uncertain about ourselves.

Bonhoeffer, like Christ, put his family in potential danger. Bonhoeffer was eventually caught by the Nazis and, like Christ, executed. But first, he wrote a book called *The Cost of Discipleship* in which he spoke of the danger of "cheap grace." "Cheap grace is the preaching of forgiveness without requiring repentance, baptism without church discipline. Communion without confession. Cheap grace is grace without discipleship, grace without the cross, grace without Jesus Christ."

That's not a formula, that's a call. And as Dietrich observed, "When Christ calls a man, he calls him to die."

Blessed Father, teach us to refrain from counting the cost.
Let the lives of those who died in your name bear fruit in me.

Saying Farewell

And [someone else] said, "I will follow you, Lord, but first let me say farewell to my family at home." [To him] Jesus said, "No one who sets a hand to the plow and looks to what was left behind is fit for the kingdom of God." (Lk 9:61-62)

The genius of the Gospels is that they address us wherever we are. They inform the way we look at our past, live in the present and, above all, ponder eternity. "For [Christ's] vitality consists in this," writes Father Hans Urs von Balthasar: "that he always stands at the level of the person he is educating and yet always is to be found as well at [as!] the final goal of his education."

The final goal of our education is always love. When you lock eyes with the person with whom you're about to fall madly, deeply, in love, you don't stop to wonder how the folks at home are going to feel. You don't pause to calculate the labor that went into those many-times-mended nets that heretofore meant your livelihood. You're not concerned with who's going to feed the ox from now on. As if in a trance, you drop the handle of the plow and start walking.

To set our hand to the plow means to begin to walk among the people of the world but with our lives based on an entirely different order from that of the world. We learn to accept scorn, betrayal, and meager results. We begin to acknowledge our deep imperfection. We become willing to accept any number of unpromising people and situations.

Not to look behind means foregoing all earthly security. But this is where things get interesting. We're given all kinds of signs to let us know when we're onto Christ, and almost the first sign is that the Way, the Truth, and the Life are *interesting*. We start to change: that's interesting. We forgive someone when we thought forgiving was impossible: that's interesting. We start to see that lack of security is not an obstacle to the path: it *is* the path.

And after awhile we're no longer tempted to look to what we left behind. We're too vitally interested in what's up ahead.

Almighty Father, teach us to keep our hand to the plow.
Teach us that to leave our family behind for your sake means to come awake to the human family in a new way.

A Just Decision

Then [Jesus] told [his disciples] a parable about the necessity for them to pray always without becoming weary. He said, "There was a judge in a certain town who neither feared God nor respected any human being. And a widow in that town used to come to him and say, 'Render a just decision for me against my adversary.' For a long time the judge was unwilling, but eventually he thought, [...] "Because this widow keeps bothering me I shall deliver a just decision for her lest she finally come and strike me.'" (Lk 18:1-5)

A child will tug and tug at his father's pants leg to get attention. A child will set up an unholy wailing in order to be heard.

But as adults, we want to appear seemly. We want to keep our desperate longing under wraps. We're embarrassed by the intensity with which we hunger for righteousness.

One of the reasons I find Saint Thérèse of Lisieux so compelling is that she was just like the importunate widow. Even as a child, Thérèse yearned to enter the cloistered convent at Carmel. So determined was she to enter at fifteen in fact—three years earlier than the minimum age—that as a teenager she cajoled her father into traveling to Rome, and on November 20, 1887, knelt at the feet of Pope Leo XIII himself.

She recounts the scene in her autobiography, *The Story of a Soul*. In spite of having been given strict orders on no account actually to speak, she pleaded: "Most Holy Father, I have a great grace to ask of you!... Most Holy Father, in honor of your jubilee, allow me to enter Carmel at the age of fifteen." The pope, startled, responded, "Well, my child, do what your superiors tell you." At which point, not satisfied with that remark, Thérèse placed her hands on his knees and in a pleading voice begged, "Oh! Most Holy Father, if you were to say yes, everyone would be willing!"… She writes, "He looked at me fixedly and pronounced these words, emphasizing each syllable: 'All right… All right… *You will enter if it is God's will.'*"

Still loath to leave without having received a definite yes, Thérèse was then taken beneath the arms by the Papal Guards, lifted up, and forcibly torn away, sobbing.

Christ knew the love required to overcome the fear of stepping outside the lines; of being considered a pest.

"Woman's will, God's will," the French say: Thérèse entered Carmel, at the age of fifteen, on April 9, 1888.

Loving Father, give us the courage to ask again and again and again. Protect us from a lukewarm, timid faith.

Faith on Earth

The Lord said, "Pay attention to what the dishonest judge says. Will not God then secure the rights of his chosen ones who call out to him day and night? Will he be slow to answer them? I tell you, he will see to it that justice is done for them speedily. But when the Son of Man comes, will he find faith on earth?" (Lk 18:6-8)

So much of life is waiting, and how impatient we are! How quick we are to think God is slow, but how slow we are to turn to trust and love him! Like the importunate widow, we beg and beg, and he showers us with gifts. The real question is: When we get what we want, what do we do with it?

I once heard a woman say, "I used to stay up all night doing crack, then lie down at 4 AM and say, 'God, please help me sleep!'" I so related. When I was in the throes of my own addiction, if I managed to get any kind of sleep, I'd get up, light a cigarette, and start drinking again.

We want God to do for us, and then to forget him. We want a magician, a miracle worker. If we really knew how little was due us, maybe we wouldn't quite so insistently ask for it. As Oscar Wilde observed in *De Profundis*, "The people who work for an hour in the vineyard in the cool of the evening receive just as much reward as those who have toiled there all day long in the hot sun. Why shouldn't they? Probably no one deserved anything."

That we don't deserve anything and yet are freely given everything is the radical basis of Christianity. Through absolutely no virtue of my own, my obsession to drink was finally lifted. I could hardly believe that my bad track record was not going to be used against me. I could start falling asleep instead of passing out. I could start seeking God and helping another alcoholic.

Christ wants not justice, but mercy. He wants us to give what we've been given away. He wants us to come awake in love.

Heavenly Father, help us to have faith. Help us call to you day and night, not with demands, but with thanks and praise.

The Rest of Humanity

[Jesus] then addressed this parable to those who were convinced of their own righteousness and despised everyone else. "Two people went up to the temple area to pray; one was a Pharisee and the other was a tax collector. The Pharisee took up his position and spoke this prayer to himself, 'O God, I thank you that I am not like the rest of humanity—greedy, dishonest, adulterous—or even like this tax collector. I fast twice a week, and I pay tithes on my whole income.'" (Lk 18:9-12)

Rules make us feel safe. Rules make us feel that, if we follow them, we get a gold star. "What would happen if everyone started bending the rules?" a certain kind of person indignantly asks. But if anyone bent the rules, it was Christ. The rule that says if you catch a woman in adultery, you gather in a circle and heave stones at her until she's dead was one of the rules Christ bent. Christ bent the rule that decreed shining up your eating vessels on the outside when he told the Pharisees: Your dishes are clean, but inside, "you are filled with plunder and evil" (Lk:11:39).

The minute we start trying to build a case for ourselves based on our perfect adherence to the law, we're in trouble. Christ reminds us that we don't get to despise anyone. We don't get to think our spiritual practice makes us one iota holier than the next person. Attending Mass in order to get a gold star avails us nothing. Fasting and tithing are meant to unite us to the rest of the world, not to separate us from it. In fact, the real fruit of the spiritual path is that we start to become more compassionate, more humble, more aware of the fact that we are not only not better than everyone else, but if anything, worse.

The cramped, rigid letter of the law crowds us up so that the only part of the church available is the front row. It fools us into thinking that we can become one with Christ without becoming one with his people.

By contrast, the expansive, resilient spirit of love opens up the whole church. Now we can sit in the front, the middle, either side, the balcony, even the back. We can mingle. We can look our brothers and sisters in the eye, and breathe freely.

Blessed Father, help us to remember that Christ came not to abolish the law but to fulfill it. Help us to remember that we are just like the rest of humanity.

The One Who Humbles Himself

"But the tax collector stood off at a distance and would not even raise his eyes to heaven but beat his breast and prayed, 'O God, be merciful to me a sinner.' I tell you, the latter went home justified, not the former; for everyone who exalts himself will be humbled, and the one who humbles himself will be exalted." (Lk 18:13-14)

One recent night a friend, disabled since birth, left a movie theater and was verbally and almost physically attacked by a gang of thugs. He was shaken, angry, and hurt. "The worst thing," he said, "was that I felt completely powerless."

At the time, I happened to have been receiving a series of anonymous hate mails on my blog. I was pretty sure I knew who the person was and my impulse was to attack back verbally. I had some information with which I could have embarrassed him. I could have "put him in his place." But listening to my disabled friend, I realized that I would then become the attacker of a person with a spiritual disability. Because clearly, people don't leave anonymous hate comments unless they feel deeply disenfranchised. People don't blindly, unreasoningly lash out at others unless they feel desperately lonely, unloved, and powerless themselves.

The truth is that we are all disabled, all broken, all wounded. That doesn't mean we allow people to hurt us. That doesn't mean we invite people to hurt us. That doesn't mean we excuse them or condone their behavior or instantly forgive them if they do hurt us.

But there is one power greater than the power of hate, and that is the power of love. The worldly rule that says the way to get ahead is by power and force was the rule that Christ utterly subverted. The worldly rule that says to hate your enemies and do everything in your power to do violence to them was the rule that Christ blew to smithereens on the cross.

Maybe the operative phrase in the passage above is "went home." Luke doesn't just say the tax collector was justified, he says he "went home" justified. Humility brings us home. Love brings us to Christ.

Dearest Father, help us be willing to stand with the tax collector in the back of the church. Help us to remember that your mercy alone allows us to live.

Let the Children Come

People were bringing even infants to [Jesus] that he might touch them, and when the disciples saw this, they rebuked them. Jesus, however, called the children to himself and said, "Let the children come to me and do not prevent them; for the kingdom of God belongs to such as these. Amen, I say to you, whoever does not accept the kingdom of God like a child will not enter it." (Lk 18:15-17)

One morning, at the conclusion of morning Mass at Saint Francis here in L.A., the priest invited the people who take the Eucharist to the sick and shut-in to come forward for a blessing. One stooped, elderly lady began to make her way toward the altar, and walking tall right behind her came a strapping gal with an infant carrier who proceeded to have a lively though inaudible conversation, right up on the steps of the altar, with the priest. This was very out of order; the alarm registered among us parishioners with much shifting of feet and clearing of throats.

"Oh, both you AND the baby!" we presently heard the priest say. "Okay, then, come any time." Then, he made the sign of the cross over their foreheads, and blessed the meek old lady, too.

I felt deeply moved by this mother with her baby who had "stepped outside the lines." Afterwards I went up to her, and she launched into a long story about how she had always loved Christ, and now she wanted to come into the Church, and her husband, who partied too much, was not interested (she herself used to steal but she was over that now), and she had two other boys besides the baby, one special-needs at the school across the street, and she was enrolled in RCIA, and she came to Mass every chance she got because she "just wanted to be with Jesus." Placing the chintzy blanket just so over little Adam, she chattered away, *beaming* with joy.

All the way home I thought, "Let the children come to me." I thought of how children don't care about making fools of themselves. Children aren't thinking of what people will say. Children don't count the cost, and plan and weigh, and draw back in fear. They just want to be loved. They just want to run toward the light. They just want to be with Jesus.

Eternal Father, give us the courage of children.
Let our hearts burn with such love that we run toward you
headlong and unheeding.

Inheriting Eternal Life

An official asked [Jesus] this question, "Good teacher, what must I do to inherit eternal life?" Jesus answered him, "Why do you call me good? No one is good but God alone. You know the commandments, 'You shall not commit adultery; you shall not kill; you shall not steal; you shall not bear false witness; honor your father and your mother.'" (Lk 18:18-20)

Christ didn't go against the structure; he went beyond the structure. But to go beyond the structure, we need first of all, for ever and always, a structure. One of the paradoxes of Christianity is that it is both utterly revolutionary and utterly practical. We never go off on a frolic of our own. We are always grounded in community, in family, in the moral law.

Just in case we're trying to veer off onto some "new" spiritual path, here's how we know whether it's valid: we don't steal, murder, lie, covet. Just in case we think we can bypass the basics and launch into some ersatz spiritual ether, let's not forget that we refrain from adultery. We remember the Sabbath and keep it holy.

To say, "It's settled: I consent to live by the teachings of the Church," affords a tremendous freedom. We voluntarily harness ourselves to the discipline and self-renunciation to which Christ, the disciples, and the saints have harnessed themselves. We begin to walk the road by which we come to the next phase: more freedom, more love. "Moving easy in harness" is how Robert Frost described the rules of poetry. And once the harness is in place we find it is guiding us where we wanted to go, perhaps unbeknownst to ourselves, all along.

When Christ asks, "Why do you call me good? No one is good but God alone," perhaps he is saying let's not forget that the highest good is love. Perhaps the supplicant, an "official," approached Christ with an air of toadying. Officials, like most of us, tend to order their lives to power, status, and prestige. Perhaps Christ was reminding us that obeying the commandments in and of itself avails us nothing. Perhaps Christ was saying: This isn't about hiding even from ourselves the gods we *really* worship. Perhaps Christ was saying that if we want to inherit eternal life, we have to be willing to allow our souls to lie stripped before the Father.

Almighty Father, help us to remember that the commandments are the solid rock on which our house is built. Help us to let our souls lie open before you.

Come, Follow Me

And [the official] replied, "All of these I have observed from my youth."
When Jesus heard this he said to him, "There is still one thing left
for you: sell all that you have and distribute it to the poor, and you
will have a treasure in heaven. Then come, follow me." But when he
heard this he became quite sad, for he was very rich. (Lk 18:21-23)

The young man was "very rich." In other words, very attached. Very afraid. Very divided.

We look for loopholes. Well, the poor, yes. A buck or two, maybe a hundred, a thousand bucks here and there, but "*all* that you have"? We like to think he meant give to the poor metaphorically—our prayers, our good thoughts. He meant that, but he also meant, in certain circumstances, for some people, at a certain stage—and oh, the discernment!—literally.

The question isn't whether Christ meant things literally or metaphorically: the question is how do we act in light of the fact that he meant everything supernaturally. Christianity is not about learning a new way to count the cost; Christianity is to stop counting the cost. Christ didn't say to give a little more than everyone else; he said to give everything. Christianity is not "balanced" or "healthy" or "sane"; Christianity is of an entirely different order. Was Saint Francis of Assisi "balanced"? Was Saint Rose of Lima, who disfigured herself to save men from being tempted by her beauty, "sane"?

Simone Weil (1909-1943), the French intellectual and mystic, took on a variety of tasks in order to be in solidarity with the poor, often with such ineptitude that she seemed to make things harder, not easier, for the folks she was trying to help. She worked on an assembly line in a factory, suffering the existential despair of a slave. She went to the front during the Spanish Civil War and stuck her foot in a pot of boiling oil. She died, possibly of self-imposed starvation.

A convert to Christ, she never officially joined the Church. That was her loss, and ours. But she also offered up her wounds, her neuroses, her weaknesses, her motives, and her body. She "sold" all that she had and distributed it to the poor.

That is more than many of us do. That is about as Catholic as you can get.

Loving Father, give us the courage to sell all that we have.
Kindle our desire to have treasure in heaven.

Possible for God

Jesus looked at [the official] [now sad] and said, "How hard it is for those who have wealth to enter the kingdom of God! For it is easier for a camel to pass through the eye of a needle than for a rich person to enter the kingdom of God." Those who heard this said, "Then who can be saved?" And he said, "What is impossible for human beings is possible for God." (Lk 18:24-27)

When "those who heard" asked, "Then who can be saved?", what did they mean? Not everybody is rich. In fact, most people aren't rich. So why did they ask, "Then who can be saved?" Maybe they meant that the people who are "favored" often seem to be the ones who have already been saved in a worldly sense. Perhaps they were asking, if being together and successful and admired in the eyes of the world doesn't give us an advantage, what does?

Christ turned any idea of a "prosperity Gospel" upside down. Blessed are the poor, not the rich. The last shall be first. That we are saved not by anything we do or earn or achieve but by the merciful love of God is a radical notion.

In one way, of course, we are all "rich." To be poor is to realize our limitations. To be poor is to realize that God doesn't protect us from our limitations: he suffers them with us. God's ways are not our ways. Neither are they senseless or absurd. But to accept God's ways means consenting to have our old ideas, our identities, and our egos continually shattered.

To help the process along, Christ often "answered" a question, as he did here, with a riddle. To the question "Then who can be saved?" Christ didn't answer, "Rich people who love God more than they love their wealth." He didn't answer,

"Poor people." He answered: "What is impossible for human beings is possible for God."

To picture a camel passing through the eye of a needle requires transcending our limited notions of time and space. Either the camel would have to be disassembled and reassembled, or the needle would have to become gigantic! The kingdom of God is not like this world, Christ tells us, but better, fairer, with more money: the kingdom of God is of a different order altogether.

Dearest Father, help us to be willing to be poor.
Help us to allow you to shatter and reassemble us,
again and again.

Giving up Our House

Then Peter said, "We have given up our possessions and followed you." [Jesus] said to them, "Amen, I say to you, there is no one who has given up house or wife or brothers or parents or children for the sake of the kingdom of God who will not receive [back] an over-abundant return in this present age and eternal life in the age to come." (Lk 18:28-30)

For years I lived in a below-market-value but beautiful apartment in a section of L.A. called Koreatown. I had Oriental and kilim rugs, paintings, icons, and crucifixes. I had French windows, hand-painted tile, a plant-filled balcony. I had a living room with crown moldings, a fireplace mantel carved with cherubs, and walls painted a contemplative gray-green. People walked in and said, "It's so you!" They said, "It's so warm!" They said, *"You'll never find another place like this."*

Something about that last remark began to irk me. Perhaps I never would, but perhaps seventeen years in any apartment—especially one that was pretty much in the ghetto—is also long enough. I'd come in some sense to believe that my identity lay in that apartment. The apartment, with its emotional weight of decades of mementoes, photos, keepsakes, and journals had become a kind of psychic albatross.

I didn't understand why, but I needed to pare down. So I sold or gave away three quarters of my belongings and set off on a six-month cross-country sabbatical. I prayed, I went to Mass, I stayed at retreat houses and hermitages. I worked through a very old wound, and when I returned to L.A., a house-share opportunity materialized before I even had to begin looking for an apartment.

I now live in a better part of town, with more peace and quiet, in a house with a huge back yard, a washer-dryer, and free Wifi. I have access to a vacation home in the desert. I'm paying less than I did in my old place. I've had to stretch myself to adjust to a roommate, and best of all, my writing has flowered.

I don't know where I'll be a year from now, but I'm pretty sure I'll be able to bear fruit there as well. Giving up our house doesn't give us more security; it gives us more faith.

Blessed Father, give us the eyes to see and ears to hear that an overabundant return comes in many forms. Help us to grow in courage so that we, too, are willing to give up houses, lands, and even family for you.

Going up to Jerusalem

Then [Jesus] took the Twelve aside and said to them, "Behold, we are going up to Jerusalem and everything written by the prophets about the Son of Man will be fulfilled. He will be handed over to the Gentiles and he will be mocked and insulted and spat upon; and after they have scourged him they will kill him, but on the third day he will rise." But they understood nothing of this; the word remained hidden from them and they failed to comprehend what he said. (Lk 18:31-34)

"They understood nothing." Not they understood only in part. Not they understood as through a glass darkly. They understood nothing. They did not understand that Christ was the fulfillment of the Old Testament law. They did not understand that he was the Savior of the world. They did not understand that he would rise and thereby vanquish death, imbue our suffering with meaning, and show us how to love each other as he loved us: by laying down his life for his friends.

He took them aside, all Twelve of them. He must have been in desperate dread of the fearsome physical agony that lay in store. He must have been bursting to impart something of the magnificent glory in which he was about to enter. He must have longed for them to say, "Oh, dearest, most sublime friend! We will stay by your side." He must have longed for them to respond, "The mystery! The wonder! Do you actually mean to say that you will rise *from the dead*?"

But nothing. After all the parables about selling all you have, and giving up house and parents and children, and humbling ourselves for the kingdom of God, they understood nothing.

He would go to his crucifixion without a single disciple understanding or believing in his mission.

Perhaps the word had to remain hidden from them. Perhaps we are only given to comprehend when we are emotionally and spiritually ready to comprehend. But one thing this passage reveals to us is the almost unbearable moral loneliness in which Christ lived—and in which we are called to live, too.

They understood nothing, yet they were his closest friends. And so on the night before he died, it was the disciples with whom he shared his last meal, the disciples whose feet he washed, the disciples, in the garden of Gethsemane, whom he asked to sit with him for an hour.

They understood nothing—and he loved them anyway. That is very good news for us.

Heavenly Father, inflame our hearts with the desire to understand Jesus, even though we never fully will. Give us the love to go up to our own Jerusalem.

Approaching Jericho

Now as [Jesus] approached Jericho a blind man was sitting by the roadside begging, and hearing a crowd going by, he inquired what was happening. They told him, "Jesus of Nazareth is passing by." He shouted, "Jesus, Son of David, have pity on me!" The people walking in front rebuked him, telling him to be silent, but he kept calling out all the more, "Son of David, have pity on me!" (Lk 18:35-39)

B ack in the late eighties, in the depths of my alcoholic drinking, I happened to be visiting some friends in Tennessee. One afternoon, I wandered outside, headed toward the woods, and sank to my knees beneath a towering pine. Ants swarmed the trunk like black stars; a clump of gray-green lichen bloomed: wondrous things I had lost the capacity to wonder about. *I'm dead inside*, I thought. *If I don't stop drinking I'm going to die.*

The very next instant I felt a force—there is no other word for it—physically pulling me down. I didn't stop to think. I opened my mouth and said: "Our Father, who art in heaven, hallowed be thy name..." I hadn't said the words since Sunday school, but there they still were, within easy reach: "Thy will be done..." "Give us this day..." "Forgive us our trespasses..."

I'd always thought of people who believed in evil as religious crackpots, but what was it but evil that I was obsessed with something that was killing me? What was it but evil when I longed with all my heart to be good, useful, loved, and was compelled to do this thing that made me feel bad, exiled, hated? "Deliver us from evil!" I implored loudly, as if speaking through a door to someone I wasn't sure was there.

"Deliver us from evil," I whispered, burying my head in my sweaty, shaking hands.

After awhile my usual self-consciousness returned. "Did I just…pray?" I thought. Then I got up, walked back across the field to the house, and mixed another pitcher of gin and tonics.

But for once, the Inner Crowd had been stilled. For once, I had braved ridicule and shouted out, "Jesus, Son of David, have pity on me!" Three months later, my family held an intervention and shipped me off to rehab. That was twenty-four years ago.

I haven't had a drink since.

Almighty Father, help us to hear the cry of our own hearts.
Give us the courage to resist both outside peer pressure
and the "peer pressure" of our inner selves.

Please Let Me See

Then Jesus stopped and ordered that [the blind man] be brought to him; and when he came near, Jesus asked him, "What do you want me to do for you?" He replied, "Lord, please let me see." Jesus told him, "Have sight; your faith has saved you." He immediately received his sight and followed him, giving glory to God. When they saw this, all the people gave praise to God. (Lk 18:40-43)

"What do you want me to do for you?" Jesus asks, and interestingly, often we don't know what we want. We know we want money, or to be admired, or for a certain person to love us, but what do we really want? What do we want Christ to do for us?

Several years ago, I embarked on a cross-country pilgrimage. I found myself in a kind of dark night of the soul, a situation I couldn't see my way out of, and so I decided to drive from Los Angeles to my childhood home of New Hampshire and back, going to Mass every day. I wanted to get closer to Christ. I knew Christ was my only answer. All I knew was to drive and stay close to Christ.

In Spencer, West Virginia, I stayed with third order Franciscan contemplative hermit Sister Jeanne McNulty. One night she made dinner and I poured out my heart, and at the end she looked at me very gently, and said, "You need to know what you want. When you know what you want, God will lead you to it. God will open the way. But you have to ask yourself, *What do I want?*"

I'd thought I knew exactly what I wanted. But I sat there for a minute, stunned, and then I said wonderingly, "I don't know what I want."

Notice, however, that the blind man didn't say, "*Make me see.*" He said, "*Let* me see." Even in his blindness, he "saw" that Christ doesn't work from the outside; he works from the inside. Saint Thérèse of Lisieux wrote, "My God, you know the only thing I've ever wanted is to love you; I have no ambition for any other glory except that."

That's a pretty good ambition for all of us. Let me see what I want. Open the eyes of my heart.

Most merciful Father, allow us to have the faith of the blind man. Lead us to ponder what we want Jesus to do for us.

In the Beginning

Was the Word:

Reflections on John

Passing through Samaria

Now when Jesus learned that the Pharisees had heard that Jesus was making and baptizing more disciples than John (although Jesus himself was not baptizing, just his disciples), he left Judea and returned to Galilee. He had to pass through Samaria. (Jn 4:1-4)

Already Christ is having to pass through unfriendly territories in order to return home. Already he is being falsely accused. Already the Pharisees are jealous of his "success."

One of the most striking things about Christ is that from the moment of his public ministry he is under siege. He never does the "safe" thing. He doesn't court danger, but neither does he try to avoid it. He doesn't go around trying to mount a preemptive defense, but when attacked, he has a ready answer. He's at home everywhere and he has no home. "Foxes have dens and birds of the sky have nests, but the Son of Man has nowhere to rest his head" (Mt 8:20).

John's head will soon be presented to Herod on a tray, and already Christ has nowhere to lay his own. The Samaritans believed their religion was the one true religion, preserved intact from prior to the Babylonian exile. They were opposed to Judaism. We go the long way around uncomfortable situations, undesirable people, potential conflict. That he has nowhere to lay his head allows Christ to walk straight into them.

We are all called to pass through Samaria. We are called to love the person who triggers us, threatens us, challenges us. We are called to interact with the poor person and the rich person, with the condemned convict and the teenager struggling with his sexual orientation, with the woman who has had an abortion, with the married father who is having an affair, with the troublesome, the annoying, the persistent, the person who is poised to refuse our help.

How clearly we can see the faults, the problems, the solution for others! Christ passes through Samaria in order to remind us how blind we are when it comes to ourselves.

Almighty Father, give me the courage to pass through Samaria. Help me be willing to explore the uncomfortable parts of myself.

It Was about Noon

So [Jesus] came to a town of Samaria called Sychar, near the plot of land that Jacob had given to his son Joseph. Jacob's well was there. Jesus, tired from his journey, sat down there at the well. It was about noon. (Jn 4:5-6)

The meeting between Christ and Mary Magdalene takes place at dawn. The meeting between Christ and the woman with the nard takes place near dinner time, at dusk. But the meeting that is about to take place between Christ and the Samaritan woman takes place at noon, in the full heat and full light of the day.

Noon is just when we do not want to meet Christ. We're tired from our own morning journey. We want to eat, to take a break from work, to gossip a bit, kvetch a bit, to congratulate ourselves, perhaps, on a job well done. We may have asked for God's help that morning, but by noon we're convinced, one more time, that we can manage on our own. By noon we secretly believe, one more time, that intelligence backed by will power will carry the day.

This is often true in the noon of our lives as well, and there's another reason we don't want to meet Christ at noon. We don't want to be subjected to the unforgiving glare. We don't want to be subjected to quite that much light.

Christ is tired. He sits down near the well that, centuries earlier, Jacob had given to his favorite son. There is a stillness here. A sense of expectation. Dust. Sun.

I often wonder what went through Christ's head at any given moment. Sitting by the well, is he rejoicing that his cousin John is baptizing so many? Is he thinking about the public life that lies before him? He who is all light would have welcomed the light. He who had no darkness would not have been afraid of too much light. Does noon for Christ, perhaps unlike for us, bring his deepest union with the Father?

His mind is too deep for us and it is also too clear, too transparent, for us. All we know is that when in the next instant a woman appears, he seems to have been thinking of her all his life.

Heavenly Father, make me as transparent as Christ.
Help me to be willing to face the light of noonday.
Allow me to stand by Jacob's well with Jesus.

"Give me a drink"

A woman of Samaria came to draw water. Jesus said to her, "Give me a drink." His disciples had gone into the town to buy food. The Samaritan woman said to him, "How can you, a Jew, ask me, a Samaritan woman, for a drink?" (For Jews use nothing in common with Samaritans.) (Jn 4:7-9)

The heart of the Kingdom of God is the face-to-face human encounter. Politics may bring superficial (if much needed) change, but transformation takes place through relationship. To need something from a poor person, a marginalized person; to be fed, walked with, shored up, encouraged, instructed, loved by a person of a different color, demographic, sexual orientation, neighborhood, religion, or country is a humbling and shattering experience. Most of us spend our lives surrounding ourselves with enough money, prestige, and friends that we can stay in our own little self-created universe. To need something so badly—companionship, directions, guidance—that we are willing to step outside our universe: that's where Christ is.

I once found myself in Spencer, West Virginia, a town of seven thousand, in the northwest part of the state. I'd spent a lot of time alone that year; voluntarily, but still, I was lonely. One Friday afternoon I read in the local paper of a covered-dish potluck at the nearby community center. I made a batch of deviled eggs, mentally reprised my best stories, and set out for the twenty-five-mile drive.

When I arrived, I found forty or so people who managed to be both totally accommodating and totally, comically, uninterested in me or my "journey." These folks didn't need another friend. They had friends. They had families, by whom they were surrounded. They weren't remotely fired up to have an existentially tormented, temporarily homeless person in their midst. And yet for that night, they saved me. They gave me a chair. They let me sit in on the conversation. They shared their food.

We tend to think religion is all about rules, but our religion is all about vulnerability. It is about relationship with people with whom we "use nothing in common." That night, I said, "Give me a drink." And the people of Appalachia gave.

Blessed Father, allow me to be stripped down to the point where I am invited to ask a stranger for food, for drink. Help me to remember that, to the Samaritan woman, Christ was a stranger.

Living Water

Jesus answered and said to [the Samaritan woman], "If you knew the gift of God and who is saying to you, 'Give me a drink,' you would have asked him and he would have given you living water." (Jn 4:10)

"How can you ask me for a drink?" the woman asks. You are a Jew and I am a Samaritan. We have nothing in common.

At the deepest level, she is asking who are you and who am I? Christ immediately meets the Samaritan woman at this deep level of their core identities. Immediately he transcends nationality, culture, religion, family, and gender and goes straight to God. He turns the question of who is doing the asking and who is doing the giving around. He says, in effect, if you knew who was saying to you, "Give me a drink," you would have asked *him* for a drink. You would have asked him for the water to slake your own thirst.

We want to make small talk. We want to be clever. We want to find out what the other person wants and decide whether and on what terms we'll give it to them. It's not far-fetched to imagine that the woman at the well was a bit of a flirt and a sexpot. It's not far-fetched to imagine that Christ very much appreciated beautiful women, and that he was the frequent recipient of their attention. He doesn't spurn female attention; he engages it and he cuts straight to the chase. He says, we're not going to play that game. He says, I'm way more interested in your spiritual well-being than that.

And yet Christ is for ever a poet and a troubadour. "He would have given you living water." He never nags or shames;

he's never a wet blanket, nor a prude, nor anything less than a full-blooded, virile man.

Impossible to imagine the story of Christ and the man at the well. The living water is a parable about the confluence of the masculine and the feminine. Here at the well he slakes the holy longing of both women and men by showing us how to love one another as he loved us.

Loving Father, make me thirst for the living water, even though I don't want to thirst. Help me to be impatient with small talk, evasion, and manipulation.

The Cistern Is Deep

[The (Samaritan) woman] said to [Jesus], "Sir, you do not even have a bucket and the cistern is deep; where then can you get this living water? Are you greater than our father Jacob, who gave us this cistern and drank from it himself with his children and his flocks?" (Jn 4:11-12)

How Christ must have loved women. How well he understood their thirst: for connection, to be cherished, to give themselves fully to a husband.

And how well he understood our feistiness! Dude, where's your bucket? That well is deep, baby! You're acting weird already and I suppose next you're gonna tell me you know more than our spiritual father, Jacob?

Jacob gave the Samaritans the physical cistern, the water that to be sure temporarily slakes thirst, that had sustained his children, and family, and animals, and the generations since. But the cistern is deep. Christ will give them another kind of water.

Christ is simultaneously utterly practical and utterly mystical. He insists upon the humble responsibilities of our daily tasks, but he never lets the merely material stand in his way. He's thirsty, but he's more thirsty to instruct this woman. He's not concerned with a bucket—a bucket is needed, but a bucket will show up one way or the other, just as when the Temple tax needs to be paid, he will casually send Peter to the lake and instruct him to throw in his line and "take the first fish that comes up. Open its mouth and you will find a coin worth twice the temple tax. Give that to them for me and for you" (Mt 17:27).

Here, as with the temple tax, he chooses water—next to air, the simplest, most essential element of our being—to illustrate. Here, as so often, he is challenged: *Who do you think you are?* Who do you think you are, coming into an alien territory and plunking down by our well? Who do you think you are: a man, speaking to a single, unchaperoned woman? Who do you think you are: in one breath asking for a drink and in the next, though you have no visible means that would enable you to get *any* water, speaking of the "living water"? But the cistern is deep. And Christ himself is the bucket.

Eternal Father, help me to remember that Christ is greater than my most cherished forebears. Help me to remember that Christ infuses even water with Life.

Eternal Life

Jesus answered and said to [the Samaritan woman], "Everyone who drinks this water will be thirsty again; but whoever drinks the water I shall give will never thirst; the water I shall give will become in him a spring of water welling up to eternal life." The woman said to him, "Sir, give me this water, so that I may not be thirsty or have to keep coming here to draw water." (Jn 4:13-15)

L ike all of us, the Samaritan woman wants to do an end run. She wants the wrong kind of miracle. She wants to be relieved of the humble duties of daily life.

In *The Reed of God*, Caryll Houselander writes of this misconception under which many of us labor. "There are many people in the world who cultivate a curious state which they call 'the spiritual life'… All the time spent in earning a living, cleaning the home, caring for the children, making and mending clothes, cooking, and all the other manifold duties and responsibilities, is regarded as wasted.

"Yet it is really through ordinary human life and the things of every hour of every day that union with God comes about."

Jesus never encourages us to avoid the duties of daily life. Instead, he imbues those duties with his supernatural love. He makes making the bed "living" making-the-bed. He makes commuting "living" commuting. He makes paying the bills "living" paying-the-bills.

Neither does he arrange things so that, once we meet him, we need never thirst again. Tradition has it that one of the seven last words of Christ himself was *Sitio*: I thirst. Christ himself thirsted, till the moment he died. We thirst and the thirst is slaked. We thirst again and Christ gives himself to us, again.

For years I thought I could reach a place beyond thirst. I thought: If only I could get through this dreadful wrong turn, if only I could heal myself from this mortifying character defect, if only I could free myself from this difficult relationship, *then* I might start to get somewhere! *Then* I could at last embark on the authentic spiritual life. Now I realize those challenges *are* the authentic spiritual life. Now I realize those difficulties are the Way and the Truth.

Eternal life springs from full participation in the present life. Every morning we are called, one more time, to pick up our bucket and trudge to the well.

Heavenly Father, help me to see that I don't have to do anything or to go anywhere extraordinary to find you. Help me to remember that you are extraordinary, not me.

You Have Had Five Husbands

Jesus said to [the Samaritan woman], "Go call your husband and come back." The woman answered and said to him, "I do not have a husband." Jesus answered her, "You are right in saying, 'I do not have a husband.' For you have had five husbands, and the one you have now is not your husband. What you have said is true." (Jn 4:16-18)

What you have said is true, in other words, but it's only the partial truth. It's the truth shaded. How easily Christ sees through our half-truths and subterfuges!

Sober alcoholics have been known to say of hitting bottom, "I was sick and tired of being sick and tired." The good news is that when we are sufficiently sick and tired of our lies, we will thirst for the whole truth. Our half-truths mask a deep and desperate hunger for connection, meaning, and love.

Christ is blunt but he's never mean. He doesn't say, "You've had five husbands and you're a harlot." He says, in so many words, "You've had five husbands and that's not working for ya, is it?" He says, "You've had five husbands and not one of them has slaked your thirst." He says, "No outside person, place, or thing is going to fix you, my beloved." He says, "Come to me, all who are weary and heavy-laden, and I will give you rest" (cf. Mt 11:28). Because nothing makes us more weary and heavy burdened than the bondage of our own addictions. To try to get outside things to fix us is a full-time, 24/7 job.

The essence of the sin of the adulterous woman was betrayal, but the essence of the woman at the well's is compulsion. We all develop strategies to promote our search for love.

Those strategies can harden into prison cells. They can become our organizing principles and our masters. Against all evidence, we come to believe that this man, or woman, will be The One; this relationship, or possession, or accomplishment will give us the validation that will make us whole. Other people can see our compulsive strategies, but we are generally blind to them ourselves.

Even when we are able to see them, we can't change on our own. We need something to replace the yawning void that ensues when we stop. We need the living water of Christ.

Almighty Father, help me to see the truth about myself
and the strategies I employ to get what I think I want.
Help me to align my will with yours.

The Hour Is Coming

The woman said to [Jesus], "Sir, I can see that you are a prophet. Our ancestors worshiped on this mountain; but you people say that the place to worship is in Jerusalem." Jesus said to her, "Believe me, woman, the hour is coming when you will worship the Father neither on this mountain nor in Jerusalem." (Jn 4:19-21)

Christ is never interested in superficial "religious" arguments. He never asks: Who are the "in" people? He never asks, Do you lean to the right or the left? He never asks, Are you among those who worship on the mountain or among those who worship in Jerusalem?

He asks questions like: Do you wash the outside of the cup, no matter how corrupt you are on the inside? Do you make a big show of praying on street corners even though you treat your wife, children, and co-workers badly? Is it more important to you to follow a rule than to help a person in need?

More and more we see the truth of the German theologian Karl Rahner's observation: "The Christian of the future will be a mystic or he will not be a Christian at all."

To be a mystic does not mean being vague; it means being very clear on who Christ is and what he calls us to. It means to be very clear that there is a law, and also very clear that Christ comes to fulfill the law by infusing it with spirit. It means to be very clear that there are rules and also very clear that the purpose of the rules is to provide a framework within which to explode in love.

Here, Christ is telling the Samaritan woman all that and more. She clearly knows "the rules" about worship and public morals. She knows she's breaking them. She assumes, perhaps, that Christ is going to lecture her.

Instead, he expands to infinity all notions of both law and spirit. He says, in so many words, When you break the rules, the wrong is that you harm yourself spiritually. He says, You feel guilty but the answer isn't to memorize the rules. The answer isn't to figure out whether the "good" people worship on the mountain or whether the good people worship in Jerusalem.

He says if you follow the rules out of love, you will enter the kingdom of heaven. He says, "Come to the living water." Come to me.

Loving Father, help me to remember that Christ was above all a prophet, ever ancient, ever new. Help me to remember that the hour is for ever coming.

The Father Seeks Such People

"You people worship what you do not understand; we worship what we understand, because salvation is from the Jews. But the hour is coming, and is now here, when true worshipers will worship the Father in Spirit and truth; and indeed the Father seeks such people to worship him. God is Spirit, and those who worship him must worship in Spirit and truth." (Jn 4:22-24)

I often wonder whether God suffers. Without in any way trying to diminish or anthropomorphize God, in particular I wonder whether he suffers the anxiety of waiting—as we do, when we seek, knock, ask. Without questioning that God knows in the end, that good will triumph, that love will reign, that Christ will take his place upon the throne, I wonder whether, like us, God doesn't know exactly how that will happen. To give people free will, it seems to me, is to consent to not know, to wait knowing *that* but without knowing *how*.

To say God knows no anxiety, it seems to me, is also to say that the same God who created man could just as well have not created him, or could have created him to be a programmed robot. It's to believe in a God for whom we play no part whatsoever in ongoing creation.

Instead, we have a very particular God: a God who pitches his tent among us, takes on human form, and knows the excruciating anxiety of death. Who laughs and loves, goes to weddings and parties, sweats tears of blood in the garden at Gethsemane, and gives us his very Body so that we can break him—knowing that we *will* break him—and eat. Who says, "I'll be with you till the end of time" but does not add "pushing you around like puppets" nor "sleeping."

I wonder if God does not contain his anxiety. I wonder if God does not consent to be stretched as far as he can possibly go, as Christ does on the cross. I wonder if he does not consent to hold the stretched-to-the-breaking-point tension, without lashing out, without transmitting the suffering, but rather in love, as a mother holds that kind of tension in labor—and is then split apart in birth. I think God knows all about waiting.

"Indeed the Father seeks such people to worship him." How patient he must be.

Blessed Father, help me to worship in Spirit and in truth.
Kindle my desire to be among the chosen. Seek me.

I Am He

The [Samaritan] woman said to [Jesus], "I know that the Messiah is coming, the one called the Anointed; when he comes, he will tell us everything." Jesus said to her, "I am he, the one who is speaking with you." (Jn 4:25-26)

S urely paradise must be very much like Southern California in early fall. Sometimes I wish those long afternoons would last for ever. One Friday near dusk last September, I decided to head out on foot to a seven o'clock Taizé prayer hour at Saint Francis of Assisi. First, though, I took a long walk, up and around the steep streets north of Sunset Boulevard, lost in thought, the air rich with the fragrance of lavender and wild fennel and sage.

Way up near the top of the hill, I ran into a shirtless man with a friendly look in his eye who was also walking. I gave him a quick once-over but he didn't seem crazy. He did have on two different colored socks—one green, one pink—and a "Legalize Weed" button pinned to his shorts, but he didn't seem crazy.

"Is this your regular walk?" he asked. "I saw you up at the crest."

"One of them," I smiled. "I'm out here all the time, wandering about."

"I live over by the Franklin Hills, but I thought I'd come over this way today. I've just had heart surgery so I have to be extra careful about getting my exercise. Beautiful, isn't it?"

We stopped and gazed out over the hills. The cypresses and palms were outlined in black, and the sky just beginning to turn pink.

"Beautiful," I agreed.

He produced a pack of Camels, lit one up, and luxuriously exhaled. "This time of year…you can see why it's called The Golden State."

I extended my hands, palms up, as if to embrace the whole world.

"We love L.A." I summarized.

It was one of those serendipitous moments of communion that are some of the sweetest fruit of the contemplative life. And all the way down the hill to church, I thought, *That was Christ. I just ran into Christ.*

Loving Father, help me to remember that anointing comes in many different forms. Open my eyes to see your love, your beauty, your joy, and your people.

The Disciples Were Amazed

At that moment [Jesus'] disciples returned, and were amazed that he was talking with a woman, but still no one said, "What are you looking for?" or "Why are you talking with her?" (Jn 4:27)

I once had a spiritual director to whom I often brought problems I was having with my own spiritual directees. "They should be a teeny bit afraid of you," she said. "They're coming to the mountain. You want to make it clear that your time is important."

Christ seems to have set this same tone with his disciples. He is their friend, but he never pretends to be their peer. They know all too well that he doesn't suffer fools gladly. They are already sufficiently well versed in the fact that his ways are not their ways not to ask "stupid" questions. They know that if Christ is talking to a woman, culturally taboo though that is, there must be a reason for it. They know the question, "What are you looking for?" is likely to bring a confounding, unanswerable counterquestion.

The disciples are amazed. As well as they know him, they are constantly amazed. Amazement is central to our faith. Dogma is essential; the problem comes when we mistake dogma for the mysterious, ever changing, vital experience that constitutes our actual lives. The problem comes when we jab our finger at the Catechism instead of consenting to feel what goes on every second in our hearts, bodies, souls, and minds. When we forget that religion is open, roomy, a mansion. There are many rooms in my Father's mansion and let's not forget it's a mansion, it's not a barracks, it's not a psych ward, it's not a jail. It's a mansion. It's a mansion we get to heal in, to learn how to love in. It's a mansion.

And it's a mansion with a surprise around every corner. The disciples know something interesting is bound to happen. They know Christ never does things idly or aimlessly or out of boredom. He is talking to a woman for a reason. They are amazed—and when we're on the right path, we're constantly amazed, too.

Eternal Father, help me to study the actions and words of Jesus closely. Help me to ask fewer questions and to keep my eyes and ears open.

Leaving Our Water Jar

The [Samaritan] woman left her water jar and went into the town and said to the people, "Come see a man who told me everything I have done. Could he possibly be the Messiah?" They went out of the town and came to him. (Jn 4:28-30)

One kind of conversion consists in the experience of discovering: I've been thinking all along that things were this way, and now I see they're that way! I thought the problem was my alcoholic husband; now I see the problem is the way I react to him! I thought I was living a life of sacrificial martyrdom; now I see I'm really afraid to break out of my egg and be fully born!

In the case of the woman at the well, the pre-conversion thought was perhaps along the lines of: *I'm just full of love and how sad for me, nothing ever works out!* The post-conversion thought is: *I'm not a victim; I'm actually kind of a predator. I'm trying to take the shortcut to love. I use men and I let them use me.*

When Christ is our companion, such thoughts don't lead to guilt or despair. They lead to wonder and joy. Because simultaneous with the discovery of who we really are comes the knowledge that we are loved, even in our blindness, even in our brokenness, even in our sin. Immediately we want more than anything to be worthy of that love. And our very next impulse is to drop our water jar, run back to town, and tell everyone in sight.

The Samaritan woman must have undergone a noticeable change for the people to have gone "out of the town and come to him." Often those of us in whom the change is less noticeable discover that no one else is nearly as interested as we are. Often we leave our water jar and no one goes out of the town and comes to see him at all. Often our own energy begins to flag. But we still get to dip deep into the cistern and to refresh ourselves once more. Even if no one seems to be listening, we still get to tell about the man who tells us "everything we have done."

Heavenly Father, help me to be ready to leave my water jar.
Help me to spread the word that Christ is the Messiah.
Help me to bring Christ into my own town.

Finishing His Work

Meanwhile, the disciples urged [Jesus], "Rabbi, eat." But he said to them, "I have food to eat of which you do not know." So the disciples said to one another, "Could someone have brought him something to eat?" Jesus said to them, "My food is to do the will of the one who sent me and to finish his work." (Jn 4:31-34)

I f the Samaritan woman leaves her jar, we can assume that she never dips it into the cistern and that Christ still hasn't gotten his drink. Which would mean that the whole time Christ is talking to the Samaritan woman he is sitting by the well tired and thirsty.

We know that Christ gives of himself fully, and the giving must leave him drained. We know from the story of the hemorrhaging woman (see Lk 8:43-48) that when she touches the hem of Christ's garment and is healed, he is aware "that power had gone out of him." We sense a certain power going out of him here. We sense that he has brought all his resources to bear and that he is gathering himself. He is thirsty, but he is replenishing himself at the Eternal Fount. He is physically hungry, but he is hungrier still to draw the woman at the well to the living water of the Father.

We have a Messiah who allows himself to be affected and changed by his encounter with the Samaritan woman. And that means he allows himself to be affected by his relationship with us. How alternately confused, frightened, bewildered, and challenged the disciples must have been. "Rabbi, eat," the disciples say, and he replies, "My food is to do the will of the one who sent me." My food is to finish his work.

What is the work that the Father began? His work is Christ, in us. Christ, who is for ever willing to encounter the stranger, the outcast, the unpromising person, place, situation. Christ, who consents to remain thirsty while giving someone else a glass of water. Christ, who does the will of the one who sent him while the world misunderstands, tries to give him things he doesn't need, and asks off-the-mark questions.

God gives us Christ to help us finish his work. Our job is to love.

Loving Father, help me to discern the will of the one who sent me. Help me to long to finish his work.

Sharing the Harvest

"Do you not say, 'In four months the harvest will be here'? I tell you, look up and see the fields ripe for the harvest. The reaper is already receiving his payment and gathering crops for eternal life, so that the sower and reaper can rejoice together. For here the saying is verified that 'One sows and another reaps.' I sent you to reap what you have not worked for; others have done the work, and you are sharing the fruits of their work." (Jn 4:35-38)

"Others have done the work." Consider all the people who go into surrounding us with food, shelter, clothing, entertainment at any given minute of our lives. The people who have grown, packaged, and shipped our food. The people who have manufactured our shirts, our iPods. The people who have written the books and blog posts and newspaper articles that we read to keep abreast and to be fed. The people who go into surrounding us with comfort, ease, and convenience within which we can do our work and shine in the eyes of our peers and the world.

In the parable of the talents (see Mt 25:14-30), the bad servant buries his talents reasoning that the "master" reaps where he does not sow. Here Christ reminds us that God is always sowing. Here, Christ teaches that, far from reaping where he doesn't sow, he allows us to reap where *we* don't sow.

We depend on others for our physical goods, but we depend on others far more than we know for our spiritual goods. How would we learn humility except by seeing others bear hardships far worse than ours with nary a shred of self-pity? How would we learn gratitude except by acknowledging that we who live in material abundance do so through absolutely no merit of our own?

In *The Shadow of the Sun*, the late Polish journalist Ryszard Kapuscinski writes of his time in Nigeria: "Many of my neighbors here have just the one thing. Someone has a shirt, someone a panga, someone a pickax. The one with a shirt can find a job as a night watchman (no one wants a half-naked guard); the one with a panga can be hired to cut down weeds; the one with a pickax can dig a ditch. Others have only their muscles to sell."

For those of us with many more than "just the one thing," how like Christ to allow us to share the glory of the harvest for work we haven't done.

Blessed Father, make me ever aware of the fruits I reap from the labor of others. Help me to be willing to share the fruits of my own labor.

The Woman Who Testified

Many of the Samaritans of that town began to believe in [Jesus] because of the word of the woman who testified, "He told me everything I have done." When the Samaritans came to him, they invited him to stay with them; and he stayed there two days. (Jn 4:39-40)

C hrist constantly stretches himself beyond his "comfort zone." Would you want to hang out with strangers for two days, eating their food, adapting to their schedule, putting up with their kids? Often we want to spread the Gospel to the ends of the earth, but on our terms. We want to sow the seed, but to people whom we handpick.

I was once asked to speak for a charismatic Catholic women's prayer group. Their approach was somewhat different than mine. A certain portion of the program was devoted to speaking in tongues. They seemed fixated upon miracles. When I got up to the microphone, several of the women gathered around, placed their hands on me, and prayed.

I did the best I could. I told my story. I said that the miracles I'd experienced tended to take place over a long period of time and after a lot of inner work. I said that a miracle for me was to refrain, for once, from the sharp retort.

Afterward, I felt like I hadn't done a very good job, or said what they wanted to hear. But then I thought, How do I know what people hear? How do I know whose heart is broken? How do I know who is struggling with an erring husband, a drug-addicted daughter, a fruitless job search?

How we long for everyone to "speak our language." To get our jokes. To have our taste. To "get" our elevated "spirituality." Such thoughts only prove we are not elevated at all—only Pharisees who are completely missing the point.

We need to remember that none of us is the keeper of miracles. We need to remember that Christ bears the fruit from us that he needs, not the fruit that we want. How do any of us know the day when we are hot, put-upon, and thirsty, and Christ himself appears to us, with his own special word, at the well? How do we know the day when we can be Christ for someone else?

Almighty Father, help my hardened, discriminatory heart.
Help me to remember that everyone is struggling,
everyone is suffering, everyone longs for a compassionate word.

Because of His Word

Many more [Samaritans] began to believe in [Jesus] because of his word, and they said to the woman, "We no longer believe because of your word; for we have heard for ourselves, and we know that this is truly the savior of the world." (Jn 4:41-42)

As a writer, how carefully I choose my words! How many hours I have spent thinking: If only I say it the *right* way, "they'll" understand! And as a Catholic convert who wrote a memoir about my stumbling journey to Christ, how my heart soared when I thought, Now all my lapsed Catholic friends will see the light! Now all my agnostic friends will see that Christ is the Great Reality! How clear I will make it, how accessible! How people will simply fall to their knees and laugh and weep and worship when they see that Christ is one of us!

Of course no one—or no one I'd hoped—saw anything. My friends politely congratulated me and never mentioned the book again. From my family—resounding silence.

There is one group I never expected to respond to my book: priests. How much we owe to priests, stumbling men like you and me, marked out for sainthood in their misunderstood, lonely office. How far they have gone toward showing me the gallantry, respect, and support that have shored up my life and my work. They are a stand-in for Christ, just as I am a stand-in for the Samaritan woman, as we continue to carry out our long conversation by the well.

Christ himself never gilds the lily. He says what needs to be said and leaves the results to God. He calls us to a church, and he knows that church will be just as broken, as exasperating, as slow to see its faults as we are. He calls us to spread the Gospel to the ends of the earth, but he never says we will live to see the harvest.

We do what we can, but in the end Christ's Word, not our word, will convert hearts. Let us stay close to him, always, and listen to his word.

Blessed Father, help me to let you choose the words.
Help us to remember that apart from you, we can do nothing.

The Sheep Gate

After this, there was a feast of the Jews, and Jesus went up to Jerusalem. Now there is in Jerusalem at the Sheep [Gate] a pool called in Hebrew Bethesda, with five porticoes. In these lay a large number of ill, blind, lame, and crippled. (Jn 5:1-3)

The ill lie at a gate. The gate has five porticoes. But this is not just any gate. It is the Sheep Gate and near it lies a pool.

We're reminded of the parable of the sheep and the goats (see Mt 25:31-46), where Christ says we will be judged "sheep"—his friends—based not on the sharpness of our eyesight or the perfection of our limbs, but on whether we were compassionate to "the least of these." In order to be authentically compassionate, it seems, we need first to offer up our own wounds to be bathed, to be baptized. We need to ask for help, get up off our mat, and wade into the pool.

The ways that we are ill, blind, lame, and crippled often prove to be an opening, a portico. My friend I'll call Peter, victim of a random shooting at the age of seventeen, has been in a wheelchair for forty-one years. He can't get up off his mat and so, with his sense of humor, his patience, his generosity of spirit, his utter lack of self-pity, he ministers from there.

But there are mats and then there are mats. Sometimes we are called to be healers by accepting that we must stay on our mat, and sometimes we are called to be healers by getting up off our mat and walking. Peter himself has picked up many mats. He picked up the mat of sobriety. He picked up the mat of caring for his aging mother, all the way up to her death.

I once asked him what time he had to start getting ready for a 12:30 PM gathering where many of us sober alcoholics and addicts regularly meet.

"10:30?" I ventured "Ten even?"

"Six," he replied.

"Six!" I pictured him laboriously rising, fixing breakfast, showering, dressing, getting into his car, driving.

"Not a minute later," he added cheerfully. "I live by minutes and inches."

An inch to the pool. A minute of love, stretching to infinity.

Dear Father, comfort the crippled, the lame, the blind.
Help us to bear our infirmities of mind and body
with patient endurance.

Wanting to Be Well

One man was there [at the pool] who had been ill for thirty-eight years. When Jesus saw him lying there and knew that he had been ill for a long time, he said to him, "Do you want to be well?" The sick man answered him, "Sir, I have no one to put me into the pool when the water is stirred up; while I am on my way, someone else gets down there before me." (Jn 5:4-7)

To suffer with our fellow wounded is a beautiful thing. Often the ill can understand one another as no one else can. But sometimes the line between compassion and pathology becomes thin. Sometimes we can get a little too comfortable by the pool. Sometimes we begin to enjoy our suffering, to identify ourselves with our suffering. Sometimes we begin to believe that we cannot get well. That belief becomes our organizing principle, and then a possession, and then a chain.

We can make efforts to get well but subconsciously the efforts can be halfhearted. Subconsciously, we can come to prefer eliciting pity or even contempt rather than shouldering the obligations of "normal" life. Subconsciously, we can become terrified of what getting well might mean. What might we be called to? What new responsibility might be ours? Who or what would we be if we were no longer *by* the pool, but *in* it along with everyone else?

A priest friend once noted that nowhere does Scripture say, "God helps those who help themselves." In fact, he pointed out, God helps those who *can't* help themselves. But you have to want to be helped. You can't be at cross-purposes with your deepest self. That in thirty-eight years not one person has come along who is willing to carry the paralytic to the pool strains credulity. "Prayer is the daily admission of one's weakness," observes Father Bernard Bro, o.p., and sometimes our deepest weakness is that we've come to prefer sickness to health.

God can work any way he sees fit. He sometimes heals us when we didn't ask to be healed and may not even particularly want to be healed. But to long to be healed, and for a long time not to be, is heartbreaking. In that case, says Christ, we can ask ourselves, "Do I truly *want* to be healed?" We can continue to pray for the willingness.

Blessed Father, don't let me get too comfortable by the pool.
Help me want to be healed. Help me to be willing to be willing.

Rise and Walk

Jesus said to [the sick man], "Rise, take up your mat, and walk." Immediately the man became well, took up his mat, and walked. Now that day was a sabbath. So the Jews said to the man who was cured, "It is the sabbath, and it is not lawful for you to carry your mat." (Jn 5:8-10)

Reading the Gospels through, it seems Christ is constantly shadowed by prying eyes, gossiping tongues, and the kind of interfering spoilsports who can't bear to see another succeed. Faultfinders, nitpickers, the people with so little life of their own that they hang out looking over other people's shoulders and taking notes.

We know these people. They wouldn't dream of missing Mass and they also wouldn't dream of actually returning a smile, or pressing a neighbor's hand at the Sign of Peace. They'll make a big show out of praying the rosary, then cut you off without a pang in the parking lot. The worst of these, and Christ knew it well, are the spiritual busybodies. These are the self-proclaimed "guardians of the faith," with their magnifying lenses and checklists, who make a cottage industry out of checking the religious "credentials" of their brothers and sisters.

Their response is never, "Praise be to God, you're walking, man!" Never, "Can I give you a hand there with your belongings?" No, these are wet blankets who can't rejoice that after thirty-eight years someone is up and running again. They purse their lips and cross their arms and, with a sour look, say, "It is the sabbath, and it is not lawful for you to carry your mat."

These are the people who, when you're struggling to stand, kick you to the ground. These are the people who will watch you writhe as they brandish their Catechism. These are the people who killed Christ.

We know these people because they are ourselves; and worst of all, they are often ourselves; criticizing and carping at and pouncing on ourselves.

Christ was never about hairsplitting or nitpicking or elevating a rule over a human being. "Rise and walk," he said. And then give a hand to the next guy who's trying to rise.

Loving Father, help me to live my own life fully.
Help me to rejoice when my neighbor is fully able
to live his or hers.

Crown of Stars:

Short Biographies

of Notable Women

in the Bible

Eve

Adam blamed Eve, and Eve blamed the serpent. G. K. Chesterton said that when he accepted Christian tradition, including the doctrine of the Fall, "I could hear bolt after bolt over all the machinery falling into its place with a kind of click of relief."

Chesterton also observed that the problem with the world is not that it is unreasonable; rather that it is "nearly reasonable, but not quite." If only Eve had turned and said, "Adam, my love, forgive me!" If only she had bowed her head before God and said, "Yes, my Lord, we were both wrong." The split in our psyche is not our "fault," and yet we must take responsibility for it. What if we tell the truth and they don't love us anymore! What if we act with integrity and they kick us out? In failing to act with integrity, we have been kicked out—have kicked ourselves out—already.

It took Mary, eons later, to look God in the eye and proclaim an unqualified "Yes!" I will not blame the serpent. I will say "Yes" to all the joy, all the pain, all the unknown. I will eat fully of the tree of life.

Sarah

Sarah is Abraham's wife and Isaac's mother. She conceives in her old age. She is afraid people will laugh at her. She has the job of mothering Isaac after his traumatic experience on the mountain.

We have to wonder: What would it do to a child to go up on a mountain with his father, ostensibly to offer sacrifice, and for the father to end up holding a knife to the child's neck? What kind of a child leaves with Abraham that morning, and what kind of a child does Abraham bring back to Sarah?

Just so, life traumatizes all of us. Like Sarah, in our old age, we are better poised to nurse the psychic wounds of others. And like Sarah, our job is to withstand the laughter of others, in spite of our suffering, and to learn to laugh at ourselves.

After Abraham comes down from the mountain, the angel of the Lord says, "Because you acted as you did in not withholding from me your beloved son, I will bless you abundantly and make your descendants as countless as the stars of the sky and the sands of the seashore" (Gn 22:16-17).

Good news for Abraham, perhaps. As for the *mother* of all these children—in her old age, no less!—we can only hope that Sarah had a sense of humor.

Hagar

Hagar is the Egyptian slave of Sarah, wife of Abraham. Sarah is barren and orders Hagar to give herself to Abraham. Hagar submits, and then conceives, after which, understandably, she "looked on her mistress with disdain" (Gn 16:4).

Then "the angel of the LORD said to her, 'Behold, you are with child, and shall bear a son; and you shall call his name Ishmael, because the LORD has given heed to your affliction'" (Gn 16:11 RSV).

The Lord gives heed to our affliction. We are sometimes up against a rock and a hard place. A move in any direction will mean suffering; any choice we make will be partly right and partly wrong. If Hagar resists her mistress, she may be put to death. If she submits, she faces humiliation, repulsion, the possibility of pregnancy, emotional entanglement, and more risks ahead.

But the spiritual path always means risk, always contains both a yes and a no. God gives us a "child"—of one sort or another—and the child will be a "wild ass of a man/ his hand against everyone" (Gn 16:12). We are given unsolvable conundrums. We are given crosses that seem impossible to bear. But we are never alone.

The Lord gives heed to our affliction.

Rachel

Rachel's life reads like a soap opera.

She is switched by her father for Leah, her older sister, on her wedding night to Jacob, after which, the "second wife," she stands by as Leah bears Jacob four sons. Unable to conceive, in frustration she gives her maidservant Bilhah to Jacob: Bilhah bears Jacob two more sons and conceives another. Finally Rachel conceives and bears her own son, Joseph.

She then flees with Jacob, Leah, Joseph, and the other children into the land of Canaan, meanwhile secreting away her father's idols. Jacob, unknowing, puts a curse on the (unknown-to-him) thief. Rachel conceives another son and, fulfilling the curse, dies in childbirth, naming her newborn Ben Oni ("son of my mourning").

> *"Then was fulfilled what had been said through Jeremiah the prophet:/ 'A voice was heard in Ramah,/ sobbing and loud lamentation;/ Rachel weeping for her children...'"*
> (Mt 2:17-18).

Instead of destroying her child, Rachel is herself destroyed in giving birth. She is connected by tradition with the slaughter of the innocents, when shortly after Christ's birth Herod orders that all the male children under the age of two be killed. She is the voice of the unborn, and she is the voice of the women whom now, as then, we seldom hear—she is the voice of their repentant mothers.

Rahab

As the Isrealites advance upon Jericho, Joshua sends two men into the city as spies. Rahab, a prostitute, takes them in and, when the king's guard comes to the door, reports that the two have fled. In fact, she has hidden them on her roof under a pile of flax stalks.

Because of her faith, Rahab understands that the parting of the Red Sea and the destruction of the Amorites by Joshua's army are signs of the living God. She tells the spies that upon hearing the news, "our hearts melted" (Jos 2:11 RSV)—which is why she undertakes the potentially fatal risk of harboring them. It's safe to assume that in this melting of her heart, she gives up her life of harlotry. When Jericho is destroyed, Rahab and her family, alone among the inhabitants of the city, are spared.

Thus, Rahab is the precursor to the woman with the alabaster ointment who waters Christ's feet with her tears. "So I tell you, her many sins have been forgiven; hence, she has shown great love. But the one to whom little is forgiven, loves little" (Lk 7:47). May our own hearts melt as well. May we water Christ's feet with tears for our own sins.

Bathsheba

Bathsheba is a legendary beauty, married to King David's head soldier Uriah. David sees her bathing one day, falls madly in lust, has her brought to him, seduces and impregnates her. So David has Uriah sent to the front lines where he will almost surely be killed (to add insult to injury, he has Uriah himself bear the message to the general who issues the order).

Uriah is duly killed in battle, and David takes Bathsheba as his wife. But God is angry. We know David says to Nathan, "I have sinned against the LORD" (2 Sm 12:13 RSV). We know Nathan answers: "The LORD…has put away your sin," but "the child that is born to you shall die" (2 Sm 12:13, 14 RSV). We know the child Bathsheba bears him does die.

We know much about David and his ensuing repentance, but very little about Bathsheba. Does she mourn Uriah? Does she chafe against the bonds of forced matrimony? All we know about Bathsheba is that she eventually bears David another son, Solomon, and that she successfully finagles to have this son, rather than one of David's sons by his first wife, named David's chief heir.

We tend to hold Bathsheba's enticing beauty against her. But for all we know the most beautiful, the most secret thing about her, was her love for her son Solomon.

The Mother with Seven Sons

In the second century before Christ, a mother and her seven sons are ordered to eat pork in violation of Hebrew dietary laws. They refuse and are brought before the Greek king, who commands his soldiers to cut out the tongue of the son who has vocally defied the rule, directs them to slice off his hands and feet, and while he is completely maimed but still breathing, orders him to be fried in a caldron. Each of the sons in turn suffers the same treatment; each, before dying, declares his fidelity to the God of Israel.

Flummoxed, the king appeals to the mother to save the last son by cajoling him, at least, into eating pork. Instead, she leans over and speaking in her native tongue, encourages him to die as nobly as his brothers had. Thus he is killed too; as is, last of all, the mother.

In *Guilt*, the British mystic and convert Caryll Houselander points out that non-believers will voluntarily suffer as long as the suffering "is for *some purpose*, used as a means to an end, but they abhor 'useless suffering.'" The person of faith, by contrast, will undergo "useless" suffering for fruits that are eternal. The believer knows that even higher than a child's life is the child's soul. Thus the follower of Christ, of whom this brave mother is a forerunner, will die for love.

Susanna

Two lecherous old voyeurs conspire to surprise Susanna at her bath and rape her. She screams and puts them off. When they threaten blackmail, saying they will falsely report having caught her in adultery, she continues to spurn their advances, and they flee.

Brought before the townspeople, the crowd believes the elders and condemns Susanna to death. But she cries aloud: "O eternal God, you know what is hidden and are aware of all things before they come to be" (Dn 13:42).

And the Lord hears her. The young Daniel steps out from the crowd, calls for a fair investigation, separates the elders, and asks each to name the kind of tree under which they had seen Susanna lying with a man. One answers a mastic and the other answers an oak: thus, they are shown to be liars and are put to death in Susanna's place.

Falsely accused, ready to die rather than compromise her integrity, a caller upon God *in extremis,* Susanna is an early Christ figure.

As well, Susanna evokes just the kind of bold, gallant, creative response in Daniel that does purity—and womanhood—proud.

Mary

Mary needs no introduction. She carries us in her womb.

One morning last Advent I was trudging to the grocery store. My heart was heavy. A friend's mother had just died, another friend was suffering from depression, a shooter had randomly opened fire earlier in the week near my neighborhood in L.A. I kept gazing hopefully at the faces of the people I passed: no response. "Hi there," I kept saying: no response. The sky was gloomy, trash littered the streets, and everyone I met looked hung-over.

Headed down a steep hill, I passed a wiry man in his mid-twenties who was headed up. Just as we passed, he looked me full in the face, smiled, and said "Good morning!" "Morning!" I smiled back, and out of nowhere came the thought: "Hail Mary, full of grace! The Lord is with thee. Blessed art thou among women, and blessed is the fruit of thy womb, Jesus…"

Never had I recognized so clearly that we are all—man, woman, and child—Mary. Never had I felt so keenly the joy of Elizabeth as she saw Mary approaching over "the hill country." Never had I seen that Christ is born, over and over again, within each of us—every time we acknowledge each other as human beings; every time we greet the morning.

Mary Magdalene

Mary Magdalene enjoys a special closeness to Christ. She is mentioned in all four of the Gospels.

She is one of the Galilean women who follow Jesus as he journeys from one town and village to another, proclaiming the Kingdom of God. She witnesses the crucifixion. She sits opposite the sepulcher and sees where Christ is laid. She brings spices to anoint him. She stands outside the empty tomb and weeps. She sees two angels in white. She runs to tell the others.

Perhaps most movingly, "When he had risen, early on the first day of the week, he appeared first to Mary Magdalene, out of whom he had driven seven demons" (Mk 16:9).

When seven demons have gone out of you, you tend to be very aware that at any moment seven, or ten, or a hundred more, could take their place. You tend to want to stay very close to Christ.

To drive out seven demons costs. To sacrifice for people tends to make us love them all the more. So maybe one of the things Mary Magdalene tells us is that the more demons Christ has driven out, the more he wants to stay close to us, too.

Mary, the Mother of James and Joses

This Mary is the mother of James the younger (traditionally, James, the son of Alphaeus; thus one of the twelve disciples) and of Joses (a "brother," i.e., possibly cousin of Christ). She is a witness to the crucifixion. She is also among the women who follow Christ from Galilee and, at dawn on the first day of the week, go to the tomb with spices in order to anoint the body.

"Who will roll away the stone?" the women ask each other. When they look up, the stone had been rolled away. As they enter the tomb, they see a young man dressed in white who tells them, "Do not be alarmed. He is risen!"

At which point "they went out and fled from the tomb, seized with trembling and bewilderment. They said nothing to anyone, for they were afraid" (Mk 16:8).

Who among us would not do the same? Like us, Mary, the mother of one of Christ's disciples, knows that she stands to be scorned and shunned. Like us, she isn't sure what she's seen, nor that she can believe what she's seen. Like us, she is afraid for herself and she also must be terribly afraid for her son.

Think of the courage to go and dress the body of the crucified one. Think of the courage to continue to stand—under the circumstances—with your son, with Christ, and with Christ's mother.

Mary, the Wife of Clopas

Mary, wife of Clopas, is mentioned just once in the Gospels. She is a witness of the crucifixion, specifically, to the wrenching moment when, from the cross, Christ turns to his mother and says, "Woman, behold, your son" (Jn 19:26), and then turns to John, "the disciple… whom he loved" (Jn 19:27), and says, "Behold, your mother" (Jn 19:27).

We, too, can stand at the foot of the cross and witness this heart-stopping intersection of hard news and good news. *I, your beloved son, am dying but I present you with another kind of son. I, your beloved friend, am dying, but here, in Mary, is sister, brother, mother, father, another kind of friend.*

We know something of the Last Supper, but it is interesting to imagine "the Next Supper": the meal on Good Friday night—for even in shock, in trauma, we still hunger. We can picture Mary, Christ's mother, John, Mary of Clopas, and some of the others at table together. Incoherent with grief, barely able to pass the plate and the cup, even so, they must have had the stirrings of the knowledge that Christ is the Way, the Truth, and the Life. Stupefied with sorrow, even then they must have realized that he had given them, in a new way, to each other.

Mary, the Mother of Mark

Peter has just escaped from prison. The angel has come in the night, loosened his chains, helped him pass the first and second guard, and let him through the iron gate leading into the city of Jerusalem.

Immediately, he goes to the house of Mary, "the mother of John who is called Mark, [i.e., Mark the Evangelist], where there were many people gathered in prayer" (Acts 12:12).

A maid goes to the gate and reports back, astonished, that it is Peter. The consensus inside the house is: "You are mad." Nonetheless, floored with joy, they admit him. He tells them of the angel, asks them to report back to James and to the brethren, and departs.

That is all one kind of miracle, but maybe another kind is that during this time of persecution, "many people gathered in prayer" together—presumably all through the night. Peter, therefore, knows just where to go. He knows where the people of faith will be gathered, and he knows that they will be praying. Perhaps Mark himself is there that night, at the house of his mother. Perhaps he is thinking of the night Peter knocked at the gate when later he will write: "Watch, therefore; you do not know when the lord of the house is coming" (Mk 13:35).

Eunice and Lois

Timothy is a beloved confidant and fellow traveler of Paul. "I recall your sincere faith," Paul writes to him, a faith "that first lived in your grandmother Lois and in your mother Eunice and that I am confident lives also in you" (2 Tm 1:5).

In the 1648 Rembrandt painting, *Timothy and His Grandmother,* Timothy is a child, lingering at Lois' ample knee as she sternly but lovingly points out a line of Scripture. She is dressed humbly, in a black head covering, a black shawl, and a long wine-colored skirt, evocative, among other things, of the rich bloodline through which Timothy receives his instruction.

At the time Paul writes his Second Letter to Timothy, he is in prison awaiting execution. Timothy, too, as bishop of Ephesus, will be martyred in his old age, dragged through the streets and stoned to death for censuring a pagan festival.

Legend has it that as he breathes his last, Timothy sees the heavens open and Christ come down with a double crown, saying, "Thou shalt receive this of my hand."

He received it first at the hand of those two great women who taught him the power and treasure of Scripture: Eunice and Lois.

Damaris

Damaris is a woman of Athens, one of the few of either gender converted by Paul's preaching in the Areopagus; her name appears nowhere else in Greek literature.

Paul is preaching the resurrection of the dead, a scandal in any era, and it is humbling to consider the unlikeliness that anyone is ever converted at all. It is humbling to remember that we go back in an unbroken line to these first few converts who were willing to believe what we want to believe but can hardly bring ourselves to believe: that death is not the end; that a lowly carpenter from the backwater of Nazareth entered human space, time, and history, and vanquished death.

I once attended a prison orientation in order to be able to share the story of my alcoholism with the inmates. For three hours the trusty went on about the hardened criminals, the crafty criminals, the criminals who would come for the coffee but not for the message. But to have broken through the prison walls yourself is to know that someone else can, too.

At the end, I raised my hand. "A hundred won't hear, but one will," I said. "That is why we come."

That is how our faith is spread, then, as now.

Paul preaches. Damaris hears.

Acknowledgments

The following texts were first published in *The Magnificat Advent Companion 2011*:
You Have Hidden These Things from the Wise and the Learned
The Voice of One Crying Out in the Desert

The following texts were first published in the *Magnificat Advent Companion 2012*:
The Miracle of the Loaves and the Fishes
The Paralytic and His Friends

The following texts were first published in *The Magnificat Lenten Companion 2012*:
Paying to the Last Penny
Christ Understood Human Nature Well

The following texts were first published in *The Magnificat Lenten Companion 2013*:
Praying in Secret
Seek and You Will Find
Woman, Where Are They?
Stealing the Contributions

The following texts are first publications:
Rejoice—and Take No Offense (to be published in *The Magnificat Advent Companion 2013*).
Leaving Our Water Jar (to be published in *The Magnificat Lenten Companion 2014*).
Led by the Spirit (to be published in *The Magnificat Lenten Companion 2014*).
Left Alone with Christ (to be published in *The Magnificat Lenten Companion 2014*).

The texts of the chapter "My Soul Doth Magnify the Lord: Reflections on Luke" were first published in: *Praying with Saint Luke's Gospel*, Magnificat, © 2012.

The texts of the chapter "In the Beginning Was the Word: Reflections on John" were first published in: *Praying with Saint John's Gospel*, MAGNIFICAT, © 2013.

The texts of the chapter "Crown of Stars: Short Biographies of Notable Women in the Bible" were first published in: *The* MAGNIFICAT *Year of Faith Companion.* © *2012*.

The following texts were first published in MAGNIFICAT (original titles in parentheses):

A Dwelling Place of God (*The Presentation*, February 2012)

A Love Affair with Paradox (*The Exaltation of the Cross*, September 2012)

A Profound Inward Light (*The Transfiguration*, August 2012)

A Religion Born of Dreams (*Epiphany*, January 2012)

A Retinue Advances (*Easter*, April 2012)

A Shower of Out-of-Season Roses (*Our Lady of Guadalupe*, December 2013)

An Acute Fever (*All Saints*, November 2012)

Bringing Life Out of Death (*The Memorial of the Guardian Angels*, October 2012)

Broken By Love (*The Visitation of the Blessed Virgin Mary*, May 2013)

Co-Equal and Co-Eternal (*The Holy Trinity*, June 2012)

Embracing the Imperfect (*Saint Vincent de Paul*, September 2013)

"I choose all!" (*Saint Thérèse of Lisieux*, October 2013)

Our Relationship to Suffering (*Ash Wednesday*, February 2013)

Pure Burning Love (*Mary Magdalene*, July 2013)

Radical Transformation (*The Conversion of Saint Paul*, January 2013)

Running Away Naked (*Mark the Evangelist*, April 2013)

The Cross of Family (*Joseph, Husband of Mary*, March 2013)

The Freedom of Heaven (*All Souls' Day*, November 2013)

The Greatest Saint (*Blessed Mary*, May 2012)

The Inebriation of Love (*Precious Blood*, July 2012)

The Invisible Made Visible (*The Annunciation*, March 2012)

The Pulse of Humanity (*Sacred Heart of Jesus*, June 2013)

The Scandal of Christianity (*Martyrdom of Saint John the Baptist*, August 2013)

True North (*Christmas*, December 2012)